The Political Economy of Privatization in Rich Democracies

The Political Economy of Privatization in Rich Democracies

Herbert Obinger, Carina Schmitt, and Stefan Traub

OXFORD
UNIVERSITY PRESS

OXFORD
UNIVERSITY PRESS

Great Clarendon Street, Oxford, OX2 6DP,
United Kingdom

Oxford University Press is a department of the University of Oxford.
It furthers the University's objective of excellence in research, scholarship,
and education by publishing worldwide. Oxford is a registered trade mark of
Oxford University Press in the UK and in certain other countries

© Herbert Obinger, Carina Schmitt, and Stefan Traub 2016

The moral rights of the authors have been asserted

First Edition published in 2016

Impression: 1

All rights reserved. No part of this publication may be reproduced, stored in
a retrieval system, or transmitted, in any form or by any means, without the
prior permission in writing of Oxford University Press, or as expressly permitted
by law, by licence or under terms agreed with the appropriate reprographics
rights organization. Enquiries concerning reproduction outside the scope of the
above should be sent to the Rights Department, Oxford University Press, at the
address above

You must not circulate this work in any other form
and you must impose this same condition on any acquirer

Published in the United States of America by Oxford University Press
198 Madison Avenue, New York, NY 10016, United States of America

British Library Cataloguing in Publication Data
Data available

Library of Congress Control Number: 2015944572

ISBN 978–0–19–966968–4

Printed in Great Britain by
Clays Ltd, St Ives plc

Links to third party websites are provided by Oxford in good faith and
for information only. Oxford disclaims any responsibility for the materials
contained in any third party website referenced in this work.

Acknowledgements

Doing comparative research in general and collecting new data in particular needs much assistance from other people. On this occasion, we would like to thank our former Bremen colleagues Philipp Schuster, Andreas Etling, and Katharina Crössmann for their huge input into the compilation of our database. In addition, we benefited from the generous support of dozens of people in ministries and companies across the world who kindly provided data and shared their knowledge with us.

Special thanks go to Frank Castles for friendship and advice as well as to our close friend Reimut Zohlnhöfer (University of Heidelberg) with whom we have collaborated on this topic for several years now. We are also grateful to the *Deutsche Forschungsgemeinschaft* for generously financing the University of Bremen's Collaborative Research Center 'Transformations of the State' (TranState) of which our research group was a part. Finally, we wish to thank an anonymous referee for helpful comments and Olivia Wells and Dominic Byatt of the Oxford University Press for their patience with this book that took almost two years longer than initially expected.

Contents

List of Figures	ix
List of Tables	xi
1. Introduction	1
2. The Emergence of Public Enterprises in Historical Perspective	6
3. Determinants of Privatization and State of the Art	26
4. Mapping the Entrepreneurial State: Data and National Trajectories of Privatization	57
5. The Determinants of Privatization: Empirical Findings	70
6. Conclusion and Outlook	94
Appendix	105
References	129
Index	141

List of Figures

4.1.	Conceptualization of formal and substantial privatization	58
4.2.	Index of public entrepreneurship in 1980 (IPEr)	62
4.3.	Change in public entrepreneurship (IPEr) between 1980 and 2007	63
4.4.	Country-specific development of public entrepreneurship (IPE)	65
4.5.	Average sector development of IPEr	66
4.6.	Country-specific sector development of IPEr	66
4.7.	Sector-specific privatization trajectories	67
5.1.	Cross-national variation of constitutional barriers	81
5.2.	A map of constitutional barriers	81
5.3.	The impact of constitutional barriers contingent upon varying control variables	83
5.4.	Marginal effects of left and conservative cabinets	88
6.1.	Product market liberalization and the spread of regulatory agencies since 1980	98
6.2.	Cumulated privatization revenues of fourteen EU member countries as a percentage of GDP, 2008–13	102

List of Tables

2.1. Subsidies paid to industry as a percentage of GDP in long-term OECD member states	22
3.1. The determinants of privatization: qualitative meta-analysis	28
4.1. Index of public entrepreneurship: revenue (IPEr)	60
4.2. Index of public entrepreneurship: employment (IPEe)	61
5.1. Index of public entrepreneurship: descriptive statistics	71
5.2. Regression on time	72
5.3. Regression on time separated by sector	73
5.4. Beta convergence: error correction models	75
5.5. Error correction models for the IPEr (revenue), separated by sector	76
5.6. Error correction models for the IPEe (employment), separated by sector	76
5.7. Constitutional barriers to privatization: components and measurement	79
5.8. Constitutional barriers to privatization in twenty OECD countries, 1980–2007	80
5.9. The impact of constitutional barriers on privatization	83
5.10. Partisan impacts on privatization	86
5.11. Interaction effects of parties and institutions on privatization	87
5.12. The diffusion of privatization policy	91
6.1. Nationalization volumes by country, 2008–12	99
6.2. Privatization revenues of fourteen EU countries, 2008–13	101
6.3. General government gross financial liabilities as a percentage of nominal GDP, 2007 vs. 2014	103
A.1. The determinants of privatization: empirical test results	105
A.2. Operationalization and data sources	126

1
Introduction

This book is concerned with the political economy of privatization in advanced democracies. With the first moves occurring in the English-speaking countries, the privatization of state-owned enterprises (SOEs) and the preceding market liberalization have been core elements of state transformation in the period stretching from the early 1980s to the advent of the global economic crisis in 2008 (Leibfried et al. 2015). Over this period, governments across the world accrued more than 1.1 trillion US dollars from divesting public enterprises, with the bulk of revenues generated in OECD (Organisation for Economic Co-operation and Development) countries (Privatization Barometer 2013: 2). This vast sum clearly suggests that privatization is a topic of high political and economic salience which deserves scholarly attention. However, despite the global turn to privatization, substantial cross-national differences in the divesture of SOEs can be observed. What are the driving forces underlying this development and what political, institutional, and economic factors account for distinct national privatization trajectories? These are the main questions we address in this volume.

Since the first major privatizations of SOEs occurred in the early 1980s (Vickers and Wright 1989; Boix 1997), the empirical analysis here covers the period between 1980 and the onset of the global economic crisis in 2008. The recent crisis provides a good opportunity for taking stock of the changing role of government in economic affairs over the past three decades. It is at least arguable that the credit crunch and the resulting recession marked a turning point as privatizations ceased, at least for the time being, and the nationalization of industrial companies and financial institutions re-emerged on the political agenda, at least in some countries. In terms of case selection, we focus on twenty democratic and wealthy long-term member states of the OECD. More recent OECD member states such as Turkey, Mexico, South Korea, or Chile are not considered because of relatively low levels of economic development and/or democratic deficits in the period under scrutiny. Moreover, we exclude the post-communist countries since the comprehensive privatizations in Central and Eastern Europe were mainly driven by the transformation from a command to a market economy in the 1990s.[1] Moreover, this economic transformation was accompanied by a shift from authoritarian rule to democracy.

While research related to the privatization of public enterprises is anything but new, the existing comparative literature on the political economy of privatization suffers from at least two major shortcomings: first, previous macro-quantitative inquiries in political science and economics have only focused on privatization measured in material terms. In contrast, formal privatization, i.e. a change of the legal status of a public company, has hitherto been neglected in comparative empirical research due to an absence of appropriate data. Since this type of privatization is of eminent relevance in the public utility sectors, an important dimension of the phenomenon under scrutiny has been widely ignored by the extant literature. In terms of the dependent variable, these studies have either examined privatization revenues, changes in the shares held by the government over time, or the sheer number of privatization deals realized. These are indicators which neither allow taking the initial size of the public sector nor new nationalizations into account. Second, most of the empirical studies in this area have treated countries as independent units. In reality, however, decisions to privatize public companies must be regarded as interdependent in the sense that policy choices made in one country affect the decision-making process in other nations. The underlying mechanisms that might trigger policy diffusion are policy learning, emulation, competition, and coercion (Holzinger and Knill 2005). In fact, the global proliferation of privatization activities in the 1980s and 1990s strongly suggests that policy diffusion and policy transfer are highly relevant in this policy area. However, the impact of policy diffusion on privatization has only been addressed by a few studies in previous quantitative research (e.g. Meseguer 2004, 2009; Schmitt 2011, 2014a; Fink 2011).

Given these shortcomings in the existing literature, the rationale for this volume is to provide a fresh look at the political economy of privatization. More specifically, our book makes a novel contribution to the existing literature in at least three respects.

First, and in contrast to all existing macro-quantitative studies, our analysis is based on a two-dimensional *conceptualization of privatization*. More specifically, two forms of privatization are distinguished, namely formal and material privatization. The concept of formal privatization is of particular importance in the public utility sectors and refers to the change of the legal status of a

---

[1] See Estrin et al. (2009) for a detailed literature review of the privatization experiences in these countries.

public company. Formal privatization is the transformation of a departmental agency or a public corporation liable to public law into a state company subject to private law such as a joint-stock company. Departmental agencies do not have an own legal personality and are subordinated to a ministry, whereas public corporations, by virtue of an own legal status and a partially commercial structure, have more autonomy in day-to-day operations than departmental agencies. However, the objectives of a public corporation are typically defined by law or statute, while a formally privatized state company is subjected to the same rules and restrictions as private companies, such as a hard budget constraint. In contrast to public corporations or departmental agencies, state companies are only responsible for the well-being of the enterprise itself. However, the state remains the unique stakeholder. Formal privatization is typically a precondition for material privatization which denotes the partial or complete sale of public shares to private investors and therefore a shift from public to private ownership.

Second, our empirical inquiry is based on *new data*. Using information provided by national ministries, the (formerly) public enterprises, regulatory agencies, national laws, and financial databases, we have compiled a new panel data set which allows mapping both the size of the public enterprise sector and its change over time as our data capture the extent of public entrepreneurship at the *national level* relative to the Gross Domestic Product (GDP). Since reliable information on the national stock of public enterprises has hitherto been lacking, our new data set offers new analytical opportunities. Information on the public sector size is, for example, a prerequisite for studying convergence of privatization policies. Moreover, our data set allows us not only to measure formal and material privatization but also to track the occurrence of new nationalizations. The latter is important because privatizations, even though representing the dominant long-term development since the 1980s, has not been the only game in town, as is, for example, evident from the huge French nationalization programme adopted by the Mitterrand Government in 1981–2. Additionally, our data set contains sector-specific information allowing us to trace the development and intensity of privatization in various sectors such as utilities and manufacturing. Overall, our new data set enables us to provide a comprehensive and nuanced picture of the development of public entrepreneurship at the national level over the past thirty years.

Moreover, we provide new data for one key determinant of privatization. By focusing on the national constitutional framework, we introduce a new institutional variable that to date has not systematically been used to elucidate cross-national differences in privatization activities. Data on national constitutional barriers to privatization were collected based on a guided questionnaire completed by experts in constitutional law in all twenty countries.

Our third contribution to the literature is that we apply spatial econometrics to assess whether *policy diffusion* accounts for national privatization pathways. More precisely, we analyse whether governments respond to the privatization policies of economically, geographically, or politically related countries.

The Structure of the Book

This book consists of six chapters. Following this introduction, Chapter 2 provides a brief historical overview of the emergence of public enterprises in the Western world up until the 1970s. Our premise is that the rationale underlying the expansion of the public enterprise sector is highly relevant to understanding its retrenchment. The chapter ends with an overview of the motives and causes that have triggered the global turn to privatization since the 1980s. Chapter 3 focuses on theory and summarizes the state of the art in the quantitative literature relating to the determinants of privatization. This chapter discusses possible domestic and international determinants of privatization that may account for the cross-national variation in privatization activities. Chapter 4 presents our new data set. We take stock of the extent of public entrepreneurship at the beginning of the period of examination. Next, by using charts and diagrams, we illustrate privatization and nationalization pathways at the national level between 1980 and 2008. Thereby, we distinguish between countries as well as sectors.

Our empirical analysis is presented in Chapter 5. This core chapter of the book presents econometric evidence and fleshes out the factors accounting for the cross-national variation of privatization intensity. In a first step, we examine similarities between national privatization trajectories. Do national privatization pathways converge and can we observe a 'race to the bottom' in terms of public ownership? Extending hitherto existing analysis of privatization and convergence processes, this chapter also focuses on the spatial and temporal structure of privatization: how did privatization spread over the OECD world and can we detect path dependencies and discontinuities? In a second step, we test the determinants of privatization discussed in Chapter 3. The econometric analyses here include estimations at both the macro- and the sector level in order to obtain a comprehensive picture of privatization activities. Chapter 6 provides a summary of our findings, deals with changes in public entrepreneurship in the wake of the financial crisis, and speculates on the future role of the state as an entrepreneur.

Overall, our empirical findings suggest that economic globalization has been a driving force underlying a massive downsizing of the public enterprise sector since 1980. Nevertheless, political parties still matter for the timing and scope of national privatization activities. A further important stimulus for restructuring public enterprises has been budgetary problem pressure which in Europe was reinforced by the fiscal constraints imposed by the Treaty of Maastricht. In terms of institutional impacts, policy-specific constitutional provisions have greater explanatory power than general institutional characteristics of a political system such as the number of veto players. These constitutional regulations are of particular importance for understanding national privatization trajectories in the public utility sectors. Finally, domestic politics and economic problem pressure are not sufficient to fully grasp cross-national differences in trajectories of privatization. Apart from supranational policy impacts in EU member states, we find that interdependencies between countries affect the policy choices of governments. Policy diffusion is most pronounced in countries which are economically interdependent, indicating again that progressive market integration left a substantial impact on economic policy making.

2

The Emergence of Public Enterprises in Historical Perspective

Arguably state-owned enterprises (SOEs) are as old as the state itself (Vernon 1979: 7). The formation of a state-owned enterprise sector occurred in several waves and the reasons for setting up SOEs are as various as the emerging patterns of public entrepreneurship in the Western world. This chapter provides a brief historical overview of the emergence of public enterprises and the underlying driving forces in the period before 1980. An historical perspective is important for understanding the rationale motivating the privatizations that occurred from the 1980s onwards and their associated modes of governance (Clifton et al. 2011; Millward 2011a). As we will see in the course of this book, the emerging pattern of government intervention in the public utility sectors since the 1980s is basically a revival of the arm's-length regulation of private undertakings that had prevailed in the 19th century. In the manufacturing arena, privatizations can be partly attributed to the fact that some of the motives that had informed the creation of public companies had become obsolete in the final decades of the 20th century.

Money for Monarchs and the Public Purse

The early move to public ownership after the formation of modern nation states was not related to ideology but can rather be attributed to the self-interest of the state and various functionalist pressures. Arguably, the oldest rationale for creating SOEs was to raise public revenues. Based on special prerogatives of the Crown, monarchs almost everywhere set up public monopolies in particular sectors in an effort to raise money for the public purse. This fiscal motive was of particular relevance for goods characterized by inelastic demand. Examples include salt, tobacco, sugar, and later alcohol monopolies dating back in part to the Middle Ages in some countries.

Moreover, playing cards or matches were subject to a government monopoly in some countries. Reaping these monopoly profits by the government was economically equivalent to taxation. Since tax-collection systems were underdeveloped in this era, fiscal monopolies represented a convenient and, compared to income tax collection, less costly way of extracting resources for the state (Clifton et al. 2003: 18–19). From the 1860s onwards, the generation of public revenues was also a reason for the nationalization of profitable private railways companies (Bogart 2009). Even today, this fiscal motive is pervasive in sectors such as petroleum, natural gas, and gambling. The Swedish state liquor monopoly established in 1914 or the German spirits monopoly still exist. Oil companies such as Statoil in Norway (where the government holds 67 per cent of the shares), Eni in Italy (government share: 30.3 per cent), or the Austrian OMV (government share: 31.5 per cent) are not only the biggest industrial enterprises in these countries but also important cash cows for the government. This holds in particular for Norway, where oil revenues are channelled into an 'oil fund'—officially labelled as the *statens pensjonsfond* or Government Pension Fund. By the end of 2012 the total value of the fund was NOK 3,961 billion (€540 billion) and the net cash flow from petroleum activities represented about 37 per cent of tax revenues over the preceding decade.[1]

The Great Transformation

Following the fiscal self-interest of monarchs, the next wave of nationalizations occurred in the wake of the fundamental transformations in economy and society caused by industrialization, urbanization, population growth, and technological change in the second half of the 19th century (Polanyi 1944). The dramatic repercussions of these changes on social and economic life and the functional requirements of the emerging industrial sector necessitated the build-up of network-based infrastructures in sectors such as gas, water, electricity, transport, and communication (Wagner 1911; Forsthoff 1938). All these network utilities share common technical properties. The most important one is a decreasing average cost function over the entire output. In this case, a single provider can deliver a service in a more efficient way by taking advantage of economies of scale. This notion of a natural monopoly was certainly an important signpost on the road to government intervention in business affairs, but one not in itself sufficient for explaining public ownership. In fact, governments were regulators rather than owners of firms as private

---

[1] Det Kongelige Finansdepartement: National Budget 2013. For a summary, see: <http://www.statsbudsjettet.no/upload/Statsbudsjett_2013/dokumenter/pdf/NBudget_2013.pdf>.

service provision was initially pervasive. In most countries, network industries were, in the first instance, operated by private companies (Millward 2011a). This holds for such distinctive sectors as railways and gas. Bogart (2009: 210) reports that, for a sample of thirty-five countries, more than 90 per cent of railways miles were owned by private companies in 1860.

Early government intervention in the network-based service sectors was typically about granting rights of way over scarce and fragmented private land, the regulation of service quality, and curbing prices and profits from the emerging private monopolists (Millward 2004). However, and largely as a result of technical limitations (e.g. in terms of transmission technology), service provision was spatially limited in the 19th century and mainly restricted to the municipality level in sectors such as electricity, gas, and water. The move from regulation to municipal ownership was initially sparked by a mixture of fiscal and social policy motives, especially in larger cities suffering from the devastating social repercussions of urbanization and industrialization (Millward 2011a). Powerful local governments relied on municipal organization for extracting revenues from profitable network industries in order to cope with the hygienic problems and rampant diseases in urban agglomerations. Building up a modern infrastructure with a view to sheltering citizens from the negative social consequences of the 'Great Transformation' was also a key impetus for the spread of municipal socialism across Europe from the 1880s onwards. However, as emphasized by Polanyi (1944), the social ramifications and functionalist pressures resulting from the 'Great Transformation' mobilized actors across the entire political spectrum in search of policy responses. For example, the municipalization of gas, electricity, and tramways in Vienna was initiated by the Christian-social mayor Karl Lueger, who also commissioned the construction of a water pipeline supplying one of the then biggest cities in Europe with fresh spring water from the Alps. In a similar vein, pollution, problems of sewage disposal, and concerns about public health in growing U.S. cities sparked municipal ownership. By 1900, more than 80 per cent of the fifty biggest cities in the U.S. had public waterworks (Galambos 2000: 282). Fiscal as well as social welfare issues also motivated the creation of local savings banks. Wengenroth (2000: 109) argues that in Germany local savings banks were established to encourage savings among low-income groups and reduce the demand for local poor relief. Similar developments occurred in the Netherlands where the attempts of left-wing liberals to protect consumers from private monopoly prices also led to the take-over of gas and electricity supply by the municipalities (Davids and van Zanden 2000: 255).

What emerged from these developments during the second half of the 19th century was a mixed ownership pattern in local infrastructure sectors with public and private companies co-existing and competing with each other.

Governments acted as owners of ventures and regulators of private business and there existed various and often complex forms of public–private co-operation. Under the French concession system, for example, private entities were entrusted by the state to manage public utilities, so that private firms delivered public services. Other services, however, were directly provided by the administration (Barjot 2011).

Unification and Consolidation of Nation-States and Empires

From the final decades of the 19th century, the formation of and the growing competition between nation-states as well as technological progress accelerated the spread of public ownership not only across countries but also from the local to the national level. Efforts to speed up political and social unification, the promotion of industrialization and economic development, and ambitions to gain control over the national territory were the most important motives. Lack of private capital was a further reason for state intervention in the building of a national infrastructure. In newly established countries, such as Italy and Germany, formerly separate regions had to be connected with transport and telecommunication services after unification. Already in the year of German unification, the *Reichspost* (Imperial Post) was established not only controlling the mail, telegraph, and telephone business, but also offering banking services in subsequent years (Wengenroth 2000: 104–5). In a similar vein, Ireland witnessed a wave of nationalizations after independence from Britain (Millward 2011b: 676). Linking disparate regions was also important for large but thinly populated countries such as the United States, Sweden, Norway, and Australia (e.g. Westlund 1998). From very early on, the U.S. federal government had been involved in the allocation of public land (handled by the Department of the Interior) and ran the postal service under the auspices of the Post Office Department established in 1829. Local governments played an active role in the construction of a transport infrastructure such as canals and harbours. In respect of railways, Bogart (2009: 217) has shown that railroad nationalization between 1860 and 1912 was more common in countries with low population density. In Australia, the Commonwealth and the state governments assumed, mainly via autonomous statutory bodies, not only control over railways, but also over ports, water and irrigation, and electricity. Building a national transport, energy, and communication infrastructure was therefore an important exercise in state- and nation-building that was sparked off by efforts to increase social cohesion, national unity, government authority, and state legitimacy. Apart from linking remote regions with the capital and internal state consolidation, colonial powers were also concerned with the maintenance of the linkages between the homeland and the colonies. Establishing effective transport and communication facilities was of particular importance for economic and diplomatic exchange between the mother country and its outposts and the overall power ambitions of the Great Powers in the age of imperialism. These motives led to growing state interference in capital-intensive sectors such as the submarine telegraph and aviation. For example, the growing involvement of the Dutch government in KLM, which eventually ended up in a government majority holding in 1927, has been linked to efforts to improve the links between the Dutch East Indies and the homeland (Davids and van Zanden 2000: 257). The Belgian carrier Sabena, founded in 1923 as a private company with a public shareholding majority and awarded with exclusive transport concessions by the government, not only linked Brussels and Léopoldville (Kinshasa), but also operated a network in the Belgian Congo (Vanthemsche 2012).

National Defence and War

Even more important were strategic concerns for national defence. In Europe, in particular, the formation of public enterprises was accelerated by growing military tensions between the Great Powers from the late 19th century onwards. Increasing nationalism and imperialistic attitudes everywhere fuelled massive war preparation efforts. The nexus between war preparation and public enterprises was reinforced by two military developments of the second half of the 19th century. First, there was a rapid progress in military technology from the 1870s onwards, which gave rise to a dramatic increase in the firepower of weaponry (Porter 1994). Second, the late 19th century witnessed the spread of mass conscription throughout continental Europe. Prussia was the first country that emulated the French people's army by introducing universal male conscription in 1814. Military defeats against Prussia motivated Austria-Hungary (1868) and France (1873) to (re-)introduce general conscription. Great Britain, by contrast, lacked universal conscription until 1916. Among the smaller states, Denmark and Switzerland introduced universal conscription in their democratic constitutions of 1848, while Finland (1870), Sweden (gradually in the 1880s), the Netherlands (1901), and Norway (1905) followed in succeeding decades. Both developments dramatically changed the nature and conduct of war. It was clear that a future military conflict between the great powers would be waged as an industrialized mass war (Porter 1994) and that continental Europe would be the hot spot of this conflict.

If military conflict occurred, millions of soldiers and all kinds of supplies would need to be quickly brought to the front-lines. Moreover, rapid mass mobilization and the maintenance of military supply chains required an effective national infrastructure and it was not least pressure from the military authorities that promoted the rapid build-up, expansion, and nationalization of a national infrastructure including railways, telegraphic communications, port facilities, and, later on, airports. In the 19th century, army commands everywhere had recognized the strategic importance of railways. In Imperial Germany, for example, the allegedly higher speed of mobilization of Germany's army by rail was a constituent element of the *Schlieffen Plan*, which aimed at avoiding a two-front war in an upcoming European military conflict. More specifically, the German General Staff planned a *Blitzkrieg* against France by concentrating the bulk of the country's armed forces in the West. After the expected swift victory, the idea was that troops should be quickly redeployed by rail to the Eastern front before Russia was able to mobilize her troops. These plans and growing military tensions literally led to an international railways race. In consequence, the total length of European track lines increased from approximately 105,000 to 290,000 km between 1870 and 1914 (Stevenson 1999: 169). Military considerations and efforts to speed up economic development led to a growing state intervention in the railways sector in countries such as Germany, Austria-Hungary, Italy, Tsarist Russia, Japan, Switzerland, Norway, Denmark, and, partly, in Sweden and France (e.g. the Paris–Orleans line). In Sweden and Norway, the army was even involved in the construction of trunk lines (Stevenson 1999: 171; Millward 2004: 5, 2011b: 682). As a result, in 1913, the state owned roughly 30 per cent of the world's railroad miles (Bogart 2009). Bogart also provides econometric evidence that the significant increase in state ownership in the railways sector between 1860 and 1912 was causally linked to the military capabilities of neighbouring countries.

Apart from transport facilities, information was imperative for military success. Modern communication technologies not only improved military communication, but also offered new opportunities for mass indoctrination and propaganda in the age of mass warfare. The telegraph was used by the armed forces for the first time during the Crimean War and the American Civil War and later became an important vehicle for calling up soldiers in case of mobilization. With growing technological progress, engineer, signal, and railway corps became important parts of the military machine. In the early 20th century, both telegraph and telephone lines were nationalized in most countries (Millward 2011a). Although there were a variety of reasons for this development, military concerns certainly represent one important factor.

In addition, the military had a strong interest in strategically important industries in manufacturing (steel, ship-building, chemical industry), mining (coal, iron ore), and energy. War preparation efforts and also the experience of war were important triggers for growing state interference in these sectors. Even in the United States, a country where SOEs at the federal level were notoriously difficult to establish, the government, through the U.S. Defence Plant Corporation, temporarily became a shareholder in strategically important sectors of heavy industry during World War II (Galambos 2000: 286). State intervention in the oil sector is another example. The nationalization of British Petroleum in 1914 was clearly related to war and motivated by efforts to secure foreign oil supply for the military. Indeed, the Great War clearly demonstrated the significant strategic importance of oil and, in the post-war period, a number of countries made strenuous efforts to seize foreign oil supplies (Noreng 1981: 133). The French government extended ownership in oil refining and oil fields in the 1920s as a consequence of the shortages experienced during the First World War (Chadeau 2000: 196). The Mussolini government established the *Azienda Generale Italiana Petroli* (AGIP) in 1926, Spain nationalized the oil company CAMPSA in 1927, and Australia created the Commonwealth Oil Refineries in 1920. Apart from defence issues, fiscal motives and lack of private capital were of importance for growing state intrusion in this sector.

Parts of the munitions industry were also traditionally under public control in many countries (e.g. Lind 2013). The degree of state intervention, however, depended on the performance of the private sector (Millward 2011a: 382). The poorer the performance, the more common was state intervention, mainly in an effort to speed up economic and military modernization. Japan after the Meiji Restoration is a case in point. By 1880, the government operated five munitions works, shipyards, ten mines, steelworks, the telegraph, and railways (Weiss 1993: 334).

A further important aspect of war preparation and military rivalry was an attempt to achieve economic self-reliance and sometimes even autarky with a view to reducing dependence on foreign capital, raw materials, and foodstuffs in time of war. Public enterprises played a great role in these plans. Perhaps the most spectacular example is the comprehensive nationalization programme by the Franco regime in Spain, which in the 1940s brought railways, telecommunications, ship-building, oil distillation, chemicals, airlines (Iberia), and engineering companies under state control (Carreras et al. 2000: 210f.).[2] The nationalizations by left governments in France in the late 1930s (arms and aircraft industry, railways) and the formation of AGIP in fascist Italy were also motivated by issues related to national defence and economic autarky. Similar considerations played a role in Nazi Germany. The establishment of the *Reichswerke Hermann Göhring* (steel, mining, munitions industry) is a case in point.

---

[2] After 1945, this approach of promoting economic autarky was continued due to the growing international isolation of the Franco regime. In consequence, the 1950s witnessed a further nationalization wave and by 1960, the state owned eight out of the country's eleven biggest companies (Carreras et al. 2000: 212–13).

During war-time, war-induced economic isolation and/or destruction typically led to shortages of foodstuffs, commodities, labour, and raw materials. Governments everywhere responded to economic scarcity with a broad set of regulatory policies including price and rent controls, wage regulation, rationing, currency controls, and the nationalization of enterprises in strategically important sectors (Porter 1994). Germany, for example, established about 200 war companies during the Great War (Wengenroth 2000: 109). Overall, the free market was increasingly replaced by economic planning during war-time giving rise to a dramatic expansion of government, a centralization of state authority, and a dwindling private business sector. In addition, this kind of 'war socialism' endowed governments with extensive experience of how to manage the economy (de Swaan 1988; Klausen 1998). In many countries this legacy of war was long-lasting.

The repercussions of war after the cessation of hostilities meant a further step on the road to public ownership. Many European countries suffered from massive war-related destruction, especially after the Second World War, when large parts of the infrastructure and many production sites were flattened by air strikes and other combat activities. To begin with, economic reconstruction of national infrastructure grids required huge injections of capital, and it was often only the state which was willing to provide guarantees for or able to raise such capital under the adverse and sometimes disastrous economic conditions characterizing the immediate post-war context. Moreover, the rebuilding and stabilization of the economy required strong government involvement in terms of planning and co-ordination. In consequence, and based on a substantial dose of pragmatism, governments launched major nationalization programmes in the immediate post-war period.[3] De Gaulle's provisional government (1944–6) nationalized the coal mines, the gas and electric power industry, Air France, Renault, several commercial banks, 36 insurance companies, and the Bank of France (Porter 1994: 169; Chadeau 2000: 188–9). In 1944, all Commonwealth countries agreed that telecommunication companies with international links should be publicly owned. In consequence, Cable and Wireless was fully nationalized in Britain in 1946 (Millward 2011b: 681). Other nationalizations implemented in Britain in the 1940s included the Bank of England, the railways, civil aviation, coal, gas, and electricity. In 1951, the government eventually assumed control of the iron and steel industry. In Australia, the airline Qantas was nationalized under the auspices of a Labour cabinet in 1947. The Scandinavian countries established a common airline, SAS, in 1946. Germany and Austria faced the problem of how to deal with the Nazi undertakings and the related reorganization of these

---

[3] War-time destruction of housing stock also led to post-war municipal and central state initiatives in increasing the public housing stock.

enterprises was significantly shaped by the Allied powers. In Germany, large parts of heavy industry, notably the munitions industry (e.g. *Reichswerke Hermann Göhring* or the *Montan Ltd*), were dismantled or restructured by the Allied powers. *Volkswagen*, another enterprise created by the Nazis, was offered for sale but no buyer was found. In consequence, the state government of Lower Saxony and the federal government stepped in by default. After the dissolution of Prussia after the war, the federal government in Bonn also inherited former (Prussian) state holdings such as VIAG (*Vereinigte Industrieunternehmungen AG*) or VEBA (*Vereinigte Elektrizitäts- und Bergwerks AG*) (Wengenroth 2000: 118–19). In contrast to the thrust towards dismantling state control initiated by the Western powers, firms in the Eastern part of the country came under Soviet control and were, in consequence, nationalized.

In Austria, the post-war national unity government socialized about seventy companies based on two Nationalization Acts passed by parliament in 1946 and 1947. These included large parts of heavy industry and mining, three banks, the electricity supply industry, and transport companies. In consequence, and similarly to France, the government controlled about 20 per cent of industrial activity in the immediate post-war period. Again, pragmatism rather than ideology was pervasive since these acts were also approved by the Christian Democrats in parliament. The main motive for this comprehensive nationalization programme was to solve the question of ownerless 'German' property that emerged during Nazi rule[4] and to avert reparation claims by the Allied forces on these German assets (Stiefel 2011: 35f).

Occupation by Nazi Germany also led to a significant expansion of SOEs in Norway. Apart from public utilities such as the post office, telecommunications, energy, and the state liquor monopoly, there existed only a few public industrial companies and most of them were related to national defence. After the end of the Second World War, the government took over shares in large companies such as Norsk Hydro and an aluminium company founded by the Nazis. These companies represented almost one-third of the stock of shares held by the government in the early 1980s (Carlsson 1988a: 198).

Economic Considerations

At least three economic reasons for public ownership are highlighted in the literature on the emergence of public enterprises (cf. Toninelli 2000: 7f). The

---

[4] There was a massive take-over of Austrian firms by Germans after the *Anschluss* in 1938 (Stiefel 2011: 33). In addition, there were considerable Nazi investments in the munitions and steel industry (e.g. the *Hermann Göhring Werke* in Linz). The Allied powers declared this change in ownership null and void already in 1942.

first and arguably most important one is related to the long- and well-established notion in economics that the network-based sectors constitute a natural monopoly. The main factors here are high fixed and sunk costs (connected to the construction of grids in the gas, electricity, and railways sectors) and economies of scale. This means that it is more efficient for a particular service to be provided by a single enterprise. Given market failure, the question then is how to cope with monopoly prices and how to secure a sufficient quantity and quality of service provision. Basically, there are two approaches for dealing with these problems and both have been utilized extensively in Western economies. With the notable exception of the United States, all Western countries have opted for public ownership of a variety of sectors in order to control prices and the quality of service provision. In particular, the early decades of the post-war era were characterized by a broad consensus concerning the public supply of what in different political and legal contexts have been called public utilities (Graham 2000), *services publics* (Auby and Raymundie 2003), or *Daseinsvorsorge* (Forsthoff 1938). In consequence, goods and services such as water, gas, electricity, telecommunications, and transport were directly provided by public enterprises. In a number of European countries, including France, public service provision was even mandated by the constitution.

The United States, by contrast, remained strongly committed to private provision and relied on a regulatory approach from the time of the establishment of the Interstate Commerce Commission in 1887 (Toninelli 2000: 12) and the adoption of anti-trust legislation including the Sherman (1890) and Clayton (1914) Acts. Public ownership, in contrast, was mainly restricted to the municipal level, with intervention at the federal tier limited to the postal service, the allocation of public land (also a business of the states), the Tennessee Valley Authority (water and electricity), and, but only temporarily, share-holding in strategically important industrial companies during the Second World War (Galambos 2000).

A second economic motivation for setting up SOEs was to promote economic modernization and economic growth as well as to enter strategic markets characterized by high-risk and large-scale capital investment. This type of industrial policy was particularly important in countries where private capital was lacking and/or for economic laggards where governments were striving to catch up to the industrially leading countries. Japan after the Meiji Restoration is a good example in the late 19th century. More recently, state-holding companies such as IRI (*Istituto per la Ricostruzione Industriale*) and ENI (*Ente Nazionale Idrocarburi*) in Italy or INI (*Instituto Nacional de Industria*) in Spain played a particularly strong role in this respect during the post-war period (Martinelli 1981; Amatori 2000; Carreras et al. 2000). The promotion of economic development also motivated the nationalizations in Greece after the end of military dictatorship in 1974 as well as those in Portugal in the wake of the Carnation Revolution. As already mentioned, SOEs also had a major role in terms of economic reconstruction after the Second World War. In numerous countries, nationalized heavy industries and public utilities supplied private undertakings with basic materials and services at low prices. Moreover, public enterprises were created to accelerate regional development or to mitigate regional imbalances. In Norway and Italy, for example, several SOEs were established in economically backward areas in an effort to create employment opportunities and to attract other firms.

Third and finally, numerous nationalizations of enterprises emerged in the wake of bail-outs enacted in periods of severe political turmoil and deep economic crisis. Over the past hundred years, such rescue operations have been repeatedly on the political agenda and were carried out by actors across the entire ideological spectrum. Apart from nationalizations related to war turbulence, the Great Depression kicked off numerous nationalizations including both industrial companies and banks. The collapse of the *Creditanstalt* in Austria in 1931, the then biggest bank in Central Europe and shareholder of many major industrial companies, led to an international banking crisis and reinforced the economic downturn in Europe. The bank was eventually rescued and nationalized by a right-wing government. In a similar vein, the fascist government in Italy created the public holding company IRI to rescue several major banks with strong links to private companies in the wake of the Great Depression. Mussolini himself described IRI 'as a clinic...for firms temporarily in trouble' (Martinelli 1981: 87–8). As a result, the Italian government became de facto the owner of a significant part of the banking and manufacturing sectors. In Germany, the central government partly nationalized the *Vereinigte Stahlwerke AG* (United Steelworks, Ltd) to prevent bankruptcy in 1932. A few years later, however, the Nazis reprivatized this huge industrial conglomerate. In Sweden, the Great Depression led to major financial problems for the private railways which, together with leftist pressure, eventually led to the complete nationalization of the railways sector in 1939 (Magnusson and Ottosson 2000: 198f.). The road system followed in 1943 (Westlund 1998: 70).

The oil shocks in the 1970s served as a further prelude to rescue operations. For example, Rover and Rolls-Royce were in severe financial difficulty and were nationalized by a Conservative government in Britain. The Swedish centre-right government bailed out several industrial companies in the late 1970s (Pontusson 1989: 133–4). In consequence, the number of employees in Swedish SOEs increased from about 208,000 in 1970 to more than 321,000 in 1982 (Carlsson 1988b: 194). Similar rescue operations in manufacturing took place in Italy, Austria, and Spain in the 1970s and 1980s. Typically, the most important reason was to mitigate or to postpone the negative effects of economic structural change and growing economic globalization on the industrial labour force. Similarly, the large-scale French nationalization programme enacted by a socialist government in the early 1980s can be understood as a strategy of domestic defence, i.e. as an attempt to shelter the French industry from international competition in a pre-emptive way and to raise employment levels (Chadeau 2000). This short-lived experiment (Hall 1986) apart, bail-outs and nationalizations fell out of favour after the late 1980s, but re-emerged on the policy agenda when the Global Financial Crisis of 2008 signalled the urgent need for economic rescue operations on an unprecedented scale.

Party Politics and Ideology

While internal and external security interests, fiscal motives, and functionalist pressures were the main drivers of public ownership, ideology was an important but, as we have seen, not the root cause of nationalization before the late 19th century. Early state ownership cannot be attributed to left ideology as '[m]uch of the drive to municipalisation predated the rise of socialism as a force in elections and predated the propagation of municipal socialism as an ideology' (Millward 2004: 12). This, however, changed in the course of the 20th century with the ever increasing representation of labour parties in government. Without any doubt the political left and the affiliated unions are ideologically most inclined to public interference in the enterprise sector. The radical left even called for the nationalization of the means of production but this option was—with the notable exception of the Soviet Union and the communist bloc—nowhere put into practice even though several social democratic parties revised their party platforms to suggest that this was their eventual goal. Arguably the most prominent example in this respect was Clause IV of the constitution of the British Labour Party (1918), which stipulated the aim 'to secure for the workers by hand or by brain the full fruits of their industry and the most equitable distribution thereof that may be possible upon the basis of the common ownership of the means of production, distribution and exchange, and the best obtainable system of popular administration and control of each industry or service'. Another example is the Marxist Linz Programme of the Austrian Social Democrats (1926) which, on the one hand, included a commitment to democracy but, on the other, propagated the nationalization of the means of production and exchange as an instrument necessary to resolve the class struggle. In both countries, however, the actual impact of the left on ownership change was weak prior to World War II. In the post-war period, many left parties underwent an ideological realignment as they abandoned traditional Marxist doctrines from their party platforms. Sweden is a case in point. Despite a passionate planning debate during the immediate post-war years, the post-war 'Social Democratic concept of socialism no longer included such traditional means as nationalization of production (and) the question of ownership was expressly subordinate to optimal productivity and efficiency' (Nybom 1993: 317). In a similar vein, Carlsson (1988b: 178f.) argues that the Social Democrats had 'no political ambition to socialise the Swedish industry. Rather, there were numerous motivations for state ownership, among them defence supplies, energy supplies and fiscal issues'. Even though the Social Democrats controlled government between 1932 and 1976, state ownership in industry remained comparatively low and it is telling that the succeeding centre-right cabinet nationalized more companies in its first three years in power than the left had done in the previous 44 years (Pontusson 1989: 133). The growth of public enterprises that occurred since the late 1960s is mainly related to mounting economic problems and efforts 'across the political spectrum to providing a strong safety net for the unemployed' (Carlsson 1988b: 193). In Norway, another country dominated by the Social Democrats in the post-war period, the size of the public enterprise sector was larger than in Sweden. However, this discrepancy is strongly related to a different war legacy and the discovery of huge oil reserves in the North Sea. As in Sweden, the roots of SOEs were thus 'not primarily ideological' (Carlsson 1988a: 200). In Greece, the PASOK government under the auspices of Andreas Papandreou dramatically expanded the size of the public sector in the 1980s. Ideology certainly played a role in this respect as the Prime Minister was a far-left socialist, but clientelism was equally important. However, Papandreou only continued in a more radical way the policy course of his Conservative predecessor, Konstantinos Karamanlis, who had launched a nationalization programme after the end of the military regime in 1974. What united the left and right in fostering state-owned enterprises was a desire to increase patronage, notably the distribution of public sector jobs among their respective constituencies of support with a view to securing re-election (Evangelopoulos 2012).

The evidence suggests that the left historically was a relevant player but hardly the sole driving force behind the emergence of state-owned enterprises, with such undertakings being established by all political groups and with a variety of motivations. Conservatives, for instance, saw a close nexus between public infrastructure and full state authority over the entire national territory and, therefore, regarded an effective infrastructure as a prerequisite for securing a strong role for the state in domestic affairs (cf. Jäger 2004: 42–5). But conservative thinkers also strongly emphasized the common purpose inherent in public utilities and their role in promoting social well-being. According to the German lawyer Ernst Forsthoff, the main purpose of public utilities, or what he has described as *Daseinsvorsorge*, was to satisfy common needs under socially appropriate conditions. In his view, *Daseinsvorsorge* should be a matter for public administration and mainly a responsibility of the communes with the main difference from private sector activities being the non-profit service provision of the public sector (Forsthoff 1938). Such ideas essentially referred back to the tradition of municipal service provision that had already emerged in response to the social upheavals caused by urbanization and industrialization in the 19th century.

It is fair to conclude that public enterprises often were already in place when the left became a powerful or even hegemonic political force after the Second World War. The dramatic expansion of the public sector during war-time mentioned earlier was a gift to the European left in pursuing its political objectives (Klausen 1998). Several post-war left governments further expanded the public enterprise sector, which became an integral aspect of interventionist economic policies after 1945. Public intrusion in economic affairs was seen as a means of guaranteeing economic stability, growth, and full employment. Sparked by the past experience of economic depression and war and framed by the related proliferation of Keynesian ideas, social democrats believed that state interference in economic affairs and generous welfare state programmes could help to smooth the business cycle and cope with the market failures inevitably inherent in capitalism. In consequence, public enterprises became key elements in the mixed and co-ordinated market economies that emerged after the war. This coincided with the preferences of trade unions which everywhere were particularly well organized in the public (enterprise) sector. State-owned enterprises often were utilized as social laboratories or employment buffers and served as a showcase and model for the private business sector. Employees of public companies variously enjoyed privileges such as life-long employment contracts, fringe benefits, or a civil servant status that was associated with higher statutory welfare benefits. A good example is France, where Renault was an industrial relations laboratory offering longer holidays, higher wages, and a strong representation of unions at the company level (Chadeau 2000: 201). SOEs were also important vehicles in left efforts to establish industrial democracy (e.g. co-determination) in the 1970s.

The Five Ms

When summarizing the brief historical overview of the emergence of public enterprises until around 1980, five reasons (the 'five Ms') deserve particular attention among the broad list of closely interrelated determinants that have driven the rise of public enterprises. These factors not only contribute to our understanding of the rise of SOEs but also serve to explain cross-national variation in the size of the public enterprise sector.

Money: The practice of using fiscal monopolies as a tax equivalent to extract resources from society is the oldest motive for establishing SOEs and one that has survived to the present day. Gambling or oil companies return significant dividends to their government owners. On the other hand, governments have had, on occasion, to raise huge funds for rescue operations. Over the past 150 years, emergency bail-outs have repeatedly been on the agenda in periods of deep economic and political crisis. The recent economic crisis is no exception.

Modernization: Economic and political modernization was a second trigger for the formation and rise of public enterprises. Technological progress permitted the establishment of a modern network-based infrastructure in sectors such as transport, energy, and communications, which was not only required for the internal consolidation of nation-states, for exercising power over the state territory and for enhancing control over colonies, but was also a crucial prerequisite for promoting economic development. The latter goal was closely wedded to the third driving factor, namely military power and warfare.

Mars: The Roman god of war is strongly connected to public entrepreneurship. To put it less metaphorically, public enterprises were to a significant extent motivated by military needs, especially after the formation of modern nation-states and in step with growing military tensions since the late 19th century. Military concerns about the speed of mobilization, effective supply chains, and supply of energy and raw materials not only account for the massive expansion of the public sphere, but also explain the cross-national variation of public ownership (Millward 2011a). More specifically, mass conscription and geopolitics explain the heavy involvement of the state in continental Europe and the lesser extent of state intrusion in Britain and its settler colonies until the Second World War. Robert Millward (2011b) has convincingly argued that military competition between hostile nation-states in continental Europe was an important trigger for public ownership. By contrast, the British homeland was protected by a huge and powerful navy. Moreover, Britain benefited from an endowment in terms of coal production and a first mover advantage in militarily important sectors such as railways and telecommunications. The United States and the Antipodes[5] were distant

---

[5] However, it has to be emphasized that public interference in economic affairs was more pronounced in the Antipodes than the British motherland. In Australia, this is related to the country's origin as a penal settlement, an associated lack of private capital, the sheer size of the national territory, and the early parliamentary success of the democratic left (the world's first majority leftist government was formed in 1910). All these factors made for greater government involvement in the provision of infrastructure services. New Zealand also maintained quite a large state-owned enterprise sector, including activities in sectors such as insurance, banking, construction, housing, forestry, trade, broadcasting, tourism, telecommunications, transportation (e.g. Air New Zealand, railways), mining, and energy production and distribution (Boston 1987: 427–8).

from the military hot spot of continental Europe. Overall, both world wars as well as civil wars, such as that in Spain, were important turning points in the history of public enterprises. Growing state involvement in the post-1945 period was closely related to economic reconstruction and was facilitated by a war-induced change in preferences favouring economic planning and co-operation which constituted the basis of the post-war compromise.

Marx: Leftist ideology was an important impetus for the nationalization of enterprises, notably during the first three-quarters of the 20th century. The radical left called for a comprehensive nationalized enterprise sector and a number of social democratic parties were to varying degrees sympathetic to SOEs. However, public entrepreneurship was by no means the exclusive preserve of the left, with Christian democratic, conservative, and even fascist parties—at various times and under various circumstances—active in establishing public companies.

Monopoly: Finally, the emergence of public utilities can be attributed to the widely shared notion that most network-based industries are, by virtue of specific cost patterns (high fixed costs), characterized by a natural monopoly. Given this situation, most governments have opted for public service provision in the post-war period.

The Golden Age and Its Demise

Public intervention in economic affairs was an essential feature of the three decades following the Second World War in most of the economically advanced OECD countries. The unprecedented enthusiasm for activist expenditure policies coupled with a growing involvement of government in economic and social affairs characterizing this period (Tanzi and Schuknecht 2000; Lindert 2004; Castles 2006) was also shared by many conservative, liberal, and Christian-democratic governments. The latter's pro-interventionist stance was arguably most pronounced in post-war Italy (Grassini 1981). In consequence, the period stretching from 1945 to the advent of the oil crises of the 1970s marked the Golden Age of the mixed economy and the welfare state. One aspect of this Keynesian post-war compromise was that airlines, railways, postal services and telecommunications, the supply of electricity and gas, as well as a broad range of local services such as waste disposal and the supply of water, were directly provided by public enterprises in most of the advanced democracies.

By means of cross-subsidization between sectors, public utilities also fulfilled social welfare functions by providing goods and services nation-wide to all citizens at reasonable prices and uniform quality irrespective of local peculiarities.[6] Based on universal service provision, the public utility sector therefore represented a sort of outer skin of the core welfare state and contributed to social cohesion across the entire state territory (Leibfried 2001). In addition to public involvement in the public utility sectors, companies in manufacturing and mining, banks and insurance were controlled by the government in a number of countries even though to varying degrees. What is more, public banks often were important shareholders of industrial companies.

State ownership in Western countries peaked in the Golden Age. Growing government activism in the enterprise sector can be demonstrated by the substantial increase in governmental transfers paid to industry during this period. The development of subsidy levels in long-term OECD member states since 1960 reveals a pattern of uninterrupted increase between 1960 and 1980 (see Table 2.1).

This steady rise in expenditure levels during the Golden Age was paralleled by an increasing cross-national dispersion. Government support to industry peaked in 1980 when subsidy levels stood at an average of around 2.4 per cent of GDP. This was also the time-point of maximum cross-national dispersion: the United States only devoted 0.35 per cent of GDP to industrial support while governmental payments to industry in Norway were a massive 5.15 per cent of GDP. After that time, a rapid decline in subsidy payments took place, accompanied by strong convergence in expenditure levels. Yet, the cutbacks in subsidies represented only one aspect of a fundamental transformation of state intervention in economic affairs. Apart from a race to the bottom in public spending on economic affairs (Obinger and Zohlnhöfer 2007), virtually all Western democracies started to liberalize markets and to divest public enterprises from the 1980s onwards (Höpner et al. 2011). This transformation of state intervention can be attributed to a series of developments that affected

Table 2.1. Subsidies paid to industry as a percentage of GDP in long-term OECD member states

Year	Mean	Standard deviation	Range	N
1960	1.32	0.95	3.18	14
1965	1.51	0.87	2.92	18
1970	1.58	0.90	3.37	19
1975	2.23	1.01	4.35	20
1980	2.37	1.14	4.80	20

Source: Obinger and Zohlnhöfer (2007: 208)

---

[6] Economic theory also offers arguments that justify this type of government intervention (Lipsey and Lancaster 1956).

all countries and gave rise to a markedly changed international political economy. More specifically, the shift to privatization and liberalization was precipitated by four common developments.

The first trigger was the economic impact of two consecutive *oil shocks* in the 1970s. The resulting stagflation was a hitherto unknown phenomenon in the immediate post-war decades that was not easily amenable to classic Keynesian policy recipes. Initially, governments responded in different ways to the economic crisis. Several and mostly left governments remained committed to expansionary fiscal policies and state intervention with public enterprises playing an important part in the crisis management strategy. As already mentioned, France witnessed a wave of nationalizations under a socialist government in the early 1980s. While this was a rather untypical and short-lived experiment, labour-hoarding in SOEs was a more common practice. Public corporations were utilized in several countries as employment buffers to prevent a further rise in unemployment. For example, the overstaffing of public enterprises was a cornerstone of 'Austro-Keynesianism', a rather unorthodox set of economic policies practised by the Social Democratic single-party government in Austria in response to the oil crises of the 1970s. While the number of jobs declined in the private sector, employment in the state-run industry increased by 2 per cent between 1973 and 1980 (Nowotny 1986: 48). Labour-hoarding in state-owned enterprises was also extensively practised in Italy, Spain, Greece, and France. Grassini (1981: 72) notes that 'no large Italian company, private or public, has been able to shut down plants in the last ten years unless it was certain that its workers would be given new jobs'. While this policy helped to cushion labour-market problems in the short run, it was a strategy which turned out to be costly in the long run as it generated inefficiencies at the firm level and required increasing public subsidies to cover losses and, therefore, contributed to rising budget deficits. By contrast, several conservative governments bade farewell to the post-war Keynesian compromise once the economic performance deteriorated in the second half of the 1970s:

> This consensual approach to economic management only remained acceptable to non-socialist parties, however, as long as growth was robust and the inflation-unemployment trade-off was at most marginal. When productivity dwindled, wages outpaced it and the general performance of the economy declined, there was no longer an incentive for them to pursue expansionary and interventionist policies. On the contrary, it became clear to conservatives that policy should be constructed mainly to discipline the private sector and restore the long-run performance of the economy by means other than demand expansion. Accordingly, non-socialist parties—first in Britain and later in European continental countries—favoured again an unimpeded market economy and a small public sector and started to develop extensive privatization programmes (Boix 1997: 479).

In particular, the secular-conservative governments that came to power in the United States and Britain launched a reorientation in economic policy that later spilled over to other advanced democracies. Government intervention was no longer seen as a problem-solving necessity but as part of the problem. Rolling back the state to its core functions, more scope for private firms, fiscal discipline, and price stability were more and more seen as the key means to seek comparative advantage in open economies and as prerequisites for unleashing economic growth. As a result, the optimistic faith in the beneficial effects of big government came to a halt in the early 1980s. Public enterprises, for example, were increasingly believed to generate efficiency losses, which, in turn, would fuel new demands for public subsidies to balance the losses accrued by these corporations. The inefficiencies of SOEs were attributed to the lack of a hard budget constraint and massive public interference in commercial decisions, such as the political appointments of managers, politically mandated ad-hoc investments, or the imposition of labour-market objectives on state-owned enterprises.[7] In consequence, formal and material privatization was increasingly seen as a panacea to overcome state failure, political patronage, perverse incentives, and a lack of managerial autonomy.

Second, *technological change* was a key trigger underlying the liberalization and privatization of network-based utilities. The massive progress in information technology rendered the notion of a natural monopoly in network-based utilities such as telecommunications meaningless. The advent of mobile phones, for example, meant that a state monopoly in the telephone market could no longer be justified as the service could now easily be provided by several companies. In addition, the development of the internet and email threatened the classic letter service of postal providers which in all long-term member states of the OECD were publicly controlled in the 1980s. Technological achievements also increased competition in the energy sector as generation, delivery, and network provision could now be separately provided.

Third, *economic globalization*, not least itself facilitated by the advancements in information technology, as well as the formation of a common market in Europe and the related tight fiscal regime enshrined in the Treaty of Maastricht, increased the pressure to liberalize markets and to privatize public companies. State-owned enterprises were exposed to growing competitive pressure and were often ill-prepared to benefit from the new opportunities of globalization. Freeing public enterprises from the constraints of state ownership and political interference in managerial activities was seen as a prerequisite for attracting foreign investment and getting access to international

---

[7] With regard to political appointments, patronage, and political interference in managerial decisions see Martinelli (1981: 90) and Grassini (1981) for Italy, Mitsopoulos and Pelagidis (2009) for Greece, and Ennser-Jedenastik (2013) and Korom (2013) for Austria.

capital markets (OECD 2003: 21). Moreover, government subsidies provided to inefficient companies undermined public finances which were increasingly constrained by the European austerity regime adopted in the early 1990s and by the growing sanctioning power of international financial markets.

Finally, the *collapse of communism* in Eastern Europe marked the end of economic regime competition between two ideologically antagonistic blocs. More specifically, it delegitimized the mixed economy in Western Europe that represented a third way between American liberalism and Soviet-style command economy during the Cold War (Obinger and Schmitt 2011). The breakdown of what could be portrayed as real socialism not only weakened the Western welfare state which secured mass loyalty during the Cold War, but also discredited public enterprises as the collapse of the planned economies was grist to the mill of those arguing that government intrusion in economic affairs would end up in economic inefficiencies and state failure. In consequence, the triumph of the market over state intervention reinforced and accelerated the spread of neo-liberal ideas that had emerged in the wake of the two oil shocks.

These developments spelled the end of the post-war consensus concerning the public provision of goods and services. In the wake of the economic stagflation of the 1970s and against the backdrop of massive technological change, economic globalization, the global spread of neo-liberal ideas, the fall of communism, and the deepening of European integration, the *market*—another 'M'—was increasingly seen as the panacea for overcoming the growing economic difficulties. This reorientation culminated from the 1980s onwards in an unprecedented wave of privatization, liberalization, and cutbacks of subsidies right across the world (OECD 2003). Particularly in the utility sectors, liberalization and privatization often went hand in hand. However, irrespective of the general thrust of this trend away from SOEs, there remain significant cross-national differences in the degree to which the state has retreated from entrepreneurial activities. Tracing and explaining this variation is the main objective of this book. The next chapter will present theoretical reflections on how cross-national differences in privatization trajectories can be explained and will provide an overview of the existing empirical literature.

3

Determinants of Privatization and State of the Art

Which factors determine privatization? Or, more precisely, how can we explain different national privatization pathways in terms of timing and depth of privatization? By timing we mean the sequence of events, beginning with the first major privatization deal, whereas depth refers to the extent of privatization as measured by changes in the public involvement in state-owned enterprises (SOEs). From a theoretical perspective, four approaches may explain the timing and depth of privatization. The key variables emphasized by these theoretical strands are (i) economic performance, (ii) actor preferences, (iii) institutions, and (iv) international influences including policy diffusion.

Functionalist theory holds that economic performance, notably economic problem pressure, forces governments to launch privatization programmes. Scholars emphasizing actor preferences argue that privatization is ultimately a political decision by governments. Hence, ideology and interests of actors matter for the scope and timing of privatization. However, the room to manoeuvre of political parties and interest groups is influenced by institutional settings which may facilitate or impede privatizations. Finally, external impacts on domestic policy making are of relevance. If we consider ideological change, globalization, and technological progress as common shocks, it is implausible to assume that privatization policies of governments are independent from one another or exclusively shaped by domestic factors. It is rather more likely that governments act strategically in an interdependent world. This idea is captured by the concept of policy diffusion. Moreover, supra- and international organizations may affect national privatization policies in several ways.

In each section of this chapter, we first briefly introduce the main theoretical arguments advanced by the proponents of the respective theoretical lenses. This is followed by a survey of the related empirical literature.

We pay our attention to comparative analyses focusing on industrialized (OECD or EU) countries but do not refer to case, single-sector, and single-country studies. A fairly large number of such studies were reviewed, for example, by Megginson and Netter (2001).[1] Comparative studies exclusively focusing on privatization in developing countries (e.g. Doyle 2012; Breen and Doyle 2013) were not included due to the different economic, political, and institutional preconditions. Studies based on 'mixed' samples of industrialized, transition, and developing countries were evaluated only with respect to those determinants that are regarded in the literature as relevant for privatization in industrialized countries. Altogether, we included in the survey eighteen studies that met these criteria without pretending completeness.

At the first moment of its occurrence in the text, each study is described in more detail. We provide information on the operationalization of the key independent variables, the indicator of privatization, the sample, the period of observation, and the research design of the study. The main focus is, of course, on the empirical findings. The empirical findings are systematically summarized in Table A.1 in the appendix to this volume. Moreover, a qualitative meta-analysis is presented in Table 3.1 on p. 28.

Economic Performance

Boix (1997), who undertook one of the first macro-quantitative studies on the determinants of privatization, points to an important aspect of the phenomenon that is easily overlooked in academic and public debates: many authors have blamed the economic malaise of the 1970s for the political turn from Keynesian to market-liberal policies. As noted in Chapter 2, the two oil crises of 1973 and 1979 set off a long-lasting phase of economic deterioration, being reflected in low GDP growth rates, rising unemployment, and high inflation rates ('stagflation'). While the general trend towards privatization may in part be attributed to these exogenous shocks and the subsequent global recessions, economic performance may also be seen as a factor shaping country-specific privatization paths during the last decades. Even in the worst years after the oil crises, when the OECD's average GDP growth rate nose-dived to 0.4 per cent (1975) and 0.1 per cent (1982), there was still a sizeable variation of growth rates among its member countries. In 1975, for instance, the standard deviation of growth rates was 3.8 per cent, with Switzerland bringing up the rear (−7.3 per cent) and Greece being the frontrunner (+6.4 per cent) of the

---

[1] See also Vickers and Wright (1989); Feigenbaum et al. (1998); Villalonga (2000); Toninelli (2000); Mayer (2006); Köthenbürger et al. (2006); Arocena and Oliveros (2012).

Table 3.1. The determinants of privatization: qualitative meta-analysis

Determinant	Hypothesis (expected sign)	No. of studies	Qualitative result (comment)
Economic performance			
GDP growth rates	Low growth promotes privatization (+)	10	Past/long-term growth: ++ Current growth: −
Public budget deficits and public debt	High deficits and debt levels promote privatization (+)	16	0/+ Maastricht Treaty: +
Unemployment	Unemployment promotes privatization (+)	1	+ (?) (only a single study, econometric issues)
Inflation	Inflation promotes privatization (+)	2	0/− (?) (only two studies, theoretical relationship unclear)
The stage of economic development	Wealthier countries privatize more (+); 'tipping point' (−/+)	9	0 (sampling problems, possible nonlinearities neglected)
Actor preferences			
Political partisanship	Left governments privatize later and less than bourgeois governments (−)	15	80s: − Later: 0 (less privatization in election years)
Interest groups	More powerful labour unions obstruct privatization (−)	5	−
Institutions			
Consensus vs. majoritarian democracy	Fragmented governments privatize later and less (−)	3	80s: − Later: 0
Veto players	More veto players hinder privatization (−)	9	0
Legal origin	Low adaptability of civil law and constitutional provisions hinder privatization (−)	3	0
Capital market development	Better developed capital markets make privatization more likely and increase revenues (+)	6	+ (questionable due to causality problem: privatization increases liquidity and liquidity promotes privatization)
Constitutional provisions	Constitutional provisions hinder privatization (−)	3	− (not in all sectors)
Initial size of SOE sector	Higher initial size is associated with higher privatization effort (+)	6	+/−
International influences			
Economic integration	Efficiency hypothesis: more integrated countries privatize more (+) Compensation hypothesis: more integrated countries privatize less (−)	11	0 (+ for financial openness with respect to public utilities sectors)
Europeanization	Europeanization promotes privatization (+)	8	+/− (sector-specific effects)
Policy diffusion	Privatization policies diffuse spatially (+)	4	++

Notes: right column: empirical studies report '++' definitely positive, '+' predominantly positive, '0' predominantly no (insignificant), '+/−' mixed, '−' predominantly negative, '− −' definitely negative impact of the respective indicators on privatization

European OECD countries.[2] Given the huge variation of macro-economic conditions across countries even in times of crisis, it is reasonable to assume that economic performance is an important determinant of national privatization pathways. In this spirit, Boix (1997: 477–8) cautions against presuming that economic problem pressure serves to 'mechanically trigger the privatization of public businesses'.

According to functionalist theory, privatization is more likely to occur in countries that are confronted with economic problem pressure such as low growth rates, high unemployment rates, and high inflation rates. The more pressing these problems are, the sooner privatization programmes start and the greater should be the extent of privatization. Governments react to these macro-economic challenges by resorting to the recommendations of supply-side economists (Zohlnhöfer et al. 2008). From this perspective, the state's influence has to be rolled back in order to restore economic growth and foster employment by creating incentives for private economic activity. Positive long-term effects on employment are also expected because resources are reallocated from heavily regulated 'old' industries like mining, steel, and shipbuilding towards more liberalized new industries and services. Belke et al. (2007) emphasize, however, that the relationship between unemployment and privatization is rather complicated. Other things being equal, the microeconomic or firm-level efficiency effect of privatization might cause more unemployment in the short run. In the long run, however, this negative impact might be offset by a positive scale effect due to rising firm or sector output. It might even happen that privatization increases unemployment prior to privatization due to an announcement or restructuring effect (on the distributional effects of privatization, see below, where we deal with labour unions' interests).

Since there is a strong correlation between growth rates and public finances, both on the revenue and on the expenditure side, many scholars argue that there is an indirect impact of poor economic growth on privatization via public budget deficits and public debt (Belke et al. 2007; Zohlnhöfer et al. 2008). Privatization, in turn, is expected to have two direct effects on public budgets. First, privatization receipts can be used to bring down current deficits. Second, privatizing inefficient firms can permanently relieve the public budget from compensating losses. Christodoulakis and Katsoulacos (1993) argue that investing privatization revenues directly into the modernization of the remaining public infrastructure is the better option than retiring public debt. The government would then not only benefit from smaller deficits of the remaining public firms, but also from higher revenues from profit taxation

---

[2] Data source: National Accounts of OECD Countries, Main Aggregates (OECD stats). Turkey exhibits an even higher growth rate (+7.2 per cent) in 1975 but is not included in our sample.

and from a smaller net employment loss. Since governments shy away from unpopular and painful fiscal measures for balancing the budget, such as expenditure cuts and tax increases, privatization has the advantage of not directly hurting someone (maybe except for some employees). On the other hand, taxpayers might have learned from past experience that privatization revenues are transitory, while their side effects due to malfunctioning regulation and deteriorating service quality are lasting. So, there might even be more opposition against the privatization of certain utilities and services than against expenditure cuts and tax increases.

GDP Growth Rates

Investigating the determinants of privatization in a sample of OECD countries,[3] Boix (1997) tests the hypothesis that weak economic performance in terms of the average annual change of per capita GDP in the two decades preceding the investigation period (1979–93) induced governments to privatize. The analysis builds on a cross-section of forty-nine governments that were in power during that period. Using an ordered probit regression model, the average growth rate is then regressed on an ordinal indicator assigning a score of 1 to governments that (re)nationalized formerly private firms and a score of 5 to governments that undertook large privatizations. The regression shows that weak long-term economic growth makes higher scores of the 'business strategy' indicator significantly more likely. The probability of privatization under a hypothetical average government in a country with only 1 per cent average annual growth is 85 per cent as compared to 41 per cent with 3 per cent average growth. It is worth mentioning that the ordered probit model controls—unlike many other cross-section analyses and panel studies that were performed later—for sample selection effects (observations on the dependent variable are censored from below zero if there are countries or governments that decide not to privatize in a given period).[4] In a second model, he regresses past average annual growth on privatization proceeds as a percentage of GDP using the same sample, here without controlling for sample-selection bias. OLS regression yields a significant negative coefficient: a decline in past long-term growth by 1 per cent gives rise to privatization revenues amounting to 1.8 percentage points of average annual GDP. Note that Boix (1997) also tests two alternative short-term measures of economic performance that turn out to be insignificant.

---

[3] The sample included all OECD member states in the 1979–92 period with over a million inhabitants (that is, excluding Iceland and Luxembourg), except for Switzerland and Turkey (missing information) and the USA (no significant public business sector).

[4] Whether a country with an already small public business sector like the USA should be excluded from the sample or not, is another—controversial—issue.

Determinants of Privatization and State of the Art

Bortolotti et al. (2001) investigate material privatization in a cross-section of forty-nine countries from all world regions using two 'quantitative' privatization indicators (number of sales, privatization revenues) and two 'qualitative' indicators (stakes sold, number of public offerings (POs) over total sales). They find a strong negative impact of average annual GDP growth on sales, revenues, and stocks, and a positive impact on POs (that disappears when they control for the size of the public sector) for the period from 1977 until 1996. Though the study provides empirical support for the importance of economic problem pressure, it involves obvious endogeneity issues. Since average growth rates and privatization indicators are calculated for the same time periods, there might be interactions between both variables. Two years later, the same authors (Bortolotti et al. 2003) provide a more sophisticated econometric analysis for a 'mixed' panel of thirty-four developing and industrial countries (excluding transition economies).[5] Current values of GDP growth are regressed on a binary variable ('major privatization observed') and two metric variables (privatization revenue, stakes sold). Probit and OLS pooled, fixed effects and random effects regression models are estimated. Yet, in none of them does the coefficient of the growth variable turn out to be statistically significant. The authors also mention the selection bias inherent in the OLS models and try to avoid the endogeneity problem by using lagged exogenous variables. Regrettably, GDP growth enters the regression without lags.

Studying the determinants of privatization in a sample of twenty-two OECD countries for the period from 1990 until 2001, Belke et al. (2007) do not find a significant impact of GDP growth (lagged by one year) on privatization revenues (normalized by average GDP). Zohlnhöfer et al. (2008) investigate the determinants of privatization in a cross-section of nineteen OECD countries from 1990 until 2000. Economic problem pressure enters as the deviation from the OECD's mean growth rate for the period of 1985–95, that is lagged by five years. The coefficient is negative and statistically significant. It is equal to −1.03 meaning that a one percentage point below-average growth rate causes privatization proceeds to increase by about 1 per cent of GDP. Schmitt (2011) is among the first scholars to investigate the international diffusion of privatization in a spatial econometric framework. She focuses on the telecommunications sector in eighteen OECD countries for the period of 1980–2007. The data are partly taken from the REST[6] database (Schuster et al. 2013), which also forms the backbone of the empirical analyses presented in the next two chapters and is described there. GDP growth rates are regressed on an 'Index of Public Involvement' measuring the relative level of public involvement in

---

[5] The sample was basically the same as in Bortolotti et al. (2001) reduced by former socialist countries.
[6] REtreat of the STate from Entrepreneurial Activities. See Schuster et al. (2013) for details.

the telecommunications sector. Schmitt (2011) uses a variety of different regression models such as spatial MLE with and without country and period fixed effects. GDP growth is statistically insignificant in most of the regressions but exhibits a negative coefficient as expected. Focusing on thirteen OECD countries, Roberts and Saeed (2012) regress annual GDP growth rates on the number of privatization deals in negative binomial regression models and on privatization revenues scaled by GDP using tobit regressions in order to control for censoring. Interestingly, GDP growth exhibits a positive sign—more prosperous countries privatize more—but the regression coefficient with regard to the number of privatization deals is insignificant. The authors conclude that their result challenges the economic-problem-pressure hypothesis.

Schuster et al. (2013) use data drawn from the REST database to analyse whether OECD countries converged with respect to their privatization policies between 1980 and 2007. They also check whether GDP growth determines privatization activities. In contrast to many of the aforementioned studies, they use two stock indicators. The first one, the Revenue Index, is the weighted revenues of all SOEs in relation to the current GDP. The second one, the Employment Index, relates the weighted share of employment in SOEs to the total national employment. Effects are tested with error correction models (ECM). GDP growth exerts a relatively weak negative influence on the Revenue Index (i.e., stronger economies privatized more) and no influence on the Employment Index. Schmitt (2014a) provides an analysis of public involvement in the public utilities sectors of fifteen European countries for the period of 1980–2007 and finds that current GDP growth has no impact on the level of public involvement.

With regard to the impact of economic growth on privatization, an interesting pattern crystallizes when taking into account the different operationalizations of GDP growth by the ten empirical studies listed in Table 3.1. Those studies resorting to past and average long-term GDP growth rates consistently find a strong positive impact of low GDP growth rates on privatization; those studies using current (ideally lagged) GDP growth rates predominately report insignificant coefficients, two of them even find a slight positive slope coefficient. Leaving aside the econometric issues involved in employing current GDP growth rates, we conclude that weak past or long-term economic performance seems to have motivated countries to privatize.[7]

---

[7] There is also some evidence, however, for a slight pro-cyclical reaction of privatization revenues on GDP growth. Given the empirical robust positive correlation between GDP growth and measures of stock market capitalization and turnover (Levine and Zervos 1998), it is a bit surprising that the positive contemporaneous correlation between privatization revenue and GDP growth presents itself so weakly. One would expect governments to align public offerings of SOEs more closely with current stock market performance.

Fiscal Problems: Budget Deficits and Public Debt

Public budget deficits and public debt as their cumulative sum have been extensively used as covariates in empirical inquiries. However, Boix (1997) finds for the 1980s that his deficit indicator, the public budget balance in the first year of a government, can neither explain the timing nor the depth of privatization in OECD countries. In contrast to this, Bortolotti et al. (2001) expect a strong impact of public deficits on privatization in their much larger sample of countries. Indeed, their deficit variable, the average public deficit in the three years before the first privatization took place (scaled by GDP), remains statistically insignificant with respect to privatization revenues. The evidence for other indicators, such as the number of privatizations, is at best weak. Brune et al. (2004) regress the budget balance (positive values denote a budget surplus) on privatization revenues using several variables and model specifications for a large sample of ninety-six countries. In the cross-section analyses, they find the expected negative impact of the budget balance (annual average 1980–5) on cumulative privatization revenues accrued between 1985 and 1989. The effect proves to be stable when controlling for data censoring by a Tobit model. In the panel analysis, one-year lags of the current budget balance are regressed on annual privatization revenues. The analysis does not provide evidence of a significant relationship, even though the coefficient shows the theoretically expected sign. Meseguer (2004) analyses the diffusion of privatization policy by means of a dynamic probit model using a sample of thirty-seven Latin American and OECD countries for the period from 1980 to 1997. Her dependent variable is the likelihood of launching a privatization programme. In what follows, we concentrate only on her OECD subsample. She does not find a significant relationship between a country's public budget deficit and its government's privatization timing.

Henisz et al. (2005) investigate privatization in the telecom and electricity sectors in seventy-one countries for the period of 1977–99 using a set of different regression techniques such as multivariate probit. The budget balance turns out to be statistically insignificant. Using one-year lags of the financial balance of the general government as a percentage of GDP, Belke et al. (2007) show public deficits to have a strong positive impact on privatization revenues in their sample of OECD countries for the period of 1990–2001. An increase of the public deficit by one percentage point increases privatization proceeds by 0.4–0.6 per cent of GDP. Similar results are obtained by Zohlnhöfer et al. (2008), who use a dummy variable in order to identify countries whose budget deficits exceeded the 3 per cent deficit criterion of the Maastricht Treaty. A large budget deficit increases privatization revenues by about 0.4 per cent of GDP or more in a sample of fourteen EU member states as well as in a sample of twenty OECD countries for the period of 1990–2000.

These results seem to confirm a conjecture by Bortolotti et al. (2001: 121) that signing the Maastricht Treaty in 1992 forced European countries to accelerate divestiture in order to meet the convergence criteria.

Fink (2011) uses event history analysis in order to identify the determinants inciting governments to privatize the national telecommunications provider in twenty-one OECD countries between 1978 and 2008. The covariate for the public deficit is found to be insignificant. Likewise for the telecommunications sector of OECD countries, Schmitt (2011) detects at best a weak negative influence of public deficits. In most regression models the respective coefficient turns out to be insignificant. When investigating additionally the railways and postal sectors, Schmitt (2013) shows that the public deficit increases the likelihood of privatization in all sectors including telecommunications. The level of public involvement in these sectors is, however, positively related to the public deficit according to Schmitt (2014a). Roberts and Saeed (2012) are among the authors who do not find a significant impact of the budget balance on privatization. Schuster et al. (2013) obtain a slight positive correlation between public deficits and changes in SOE employment that disappears once country fixed effects are used.

While the aforementioned studies focus on the public budget deficit, Bortolotti et al. (2003), Bortolotti and Pinotti (2008), Schneider and Häge (2008), and Schuster et al. (2013) examine the impact of the level of public debt on privatization. Bortolotti et al. (2003: 318–19) conclude that the Maastricht Treaty's 60 per cent debt criterion has promoted privatization. This hypothesis is tested for a sample of thirty-four countries for the period from 1977 to 1999. The study actually reveals that high levels of public debt make major privatization deals more likely. However, neither privatization returns nor the size of the stakes sold are affected by public debt. Likewise, in their event history analysis of privatization timing in OECD countries, Bortolotti and Pinotti (2008) do not find a significant impact of public debt. This result is corroborated by Schneider and Häge (2008), who study the impact of a country's maximum indebtedness as a percentage of GDP on the privatization of the public infrastructure companies in twenty OECD countries between 1983 and 2000. The only study reporting unambiguously significant results is Schuster et al. (2013), who find a strong negative impact of public debt on the Revenue Index and also a weaker negative impact on the Employment Index. Hence, they conclude that higher levels of public debt have led to a retreat of the state from entrepreneurial activities both in terms of SOE revenues and employment.

Altogether, the empirical evidence regarding public budget deficits and public debt as catalysts of privatization is not particularly compelling. We conclude, however, that even though the budget constraint imposed by the Maastricht Treaty has proven to be rather soft, it might have induced heavily indebted countries to rely on privatizations more extensively than other countries exhibiting public budget deficits.

Unemployment

Belke et al. (2007) is the only study taking a look at the unemployment rate. Interestingly, this study reveals a strong and stable positive impact of the unemployment rate (lagged by one year) on privatization. An increase in the unemployment rate by one percentage point increases privatization proceeds by up to 0.12 per cent of GDP. This result raises the question whether unemployment is a better indicator of economic performance than the growth rate itself (which is insignificant). On the one hand, leaving out unemployment may lead to an omitted variable bias. On the other hand, including both growth rate and unemployment rate into the same regression equation may lead to multicollinearity problems. Unfortunately, the authors do not provide correlations between the exogenous variables or auxiliary regressions including only the growth rate or the unemployment rate, respectively. They conclude: 'differences in privatization proceeds... can primarily [be] traced back to the specific economic problems these countries face. This appears to be especially the case if the degree of problem pressure is measured by the unemployment rate, but also if the general government financial balance is considered' (Belke et al. 2007: 237).

Inflation

The effect of inflation on privatization is investigated by two studies. Meseguer (2004) obtains an insignificant coefficient for the inflation rate. Roberts and Saeed (2012) report a negative coefficient for the impact of the inflation rate on privatization revenues scaled by GDP, but provide neither a theoretical explanation nor an interpretation of their empirical result. Like Meseguer (2004), Roberts and Saeed (2012) do not only investigate OECD countries but also two samples of developing and transition countries. For once it might be worthwhile to make a short excursion to privatization studies focusing on non-OECD countries where (hyper-)inflation is much more common. For example, Doyle (2012) and Breen and Doyle (2013) investigate Latin American and developing countries using the usual set of privatization determinants. In contrast to Roberts and Saeed's (2012) OECD sample, many of these countries suffered from episodes of high inflation (see, for example, Loungani and Swagel 2001). Hence, controlling for inflation rates seems to be appropriate. Breen and Doyle (2013: 10) hypothesize that 'a high level of inflation will prompt the state to divest public assets to combat economic malaise'. It is far from obvious, however, why such a negative causal relationship between inflation and privatization should exist. In fact, there are good theoretical counter-arguments. The so-called Social View of privatization (Shapiro and Willig 1990) holds that privatization may come at the social cost of higher price levels due to monopoly power in poorly regulated industries. LaPorta and López-Silanes (1999) tested the Social View and found a moderate price increase in the Mexican economy due to privatization in the 1983–91 period. Saal and Parker (2001) demonstrate that the privatization of the water and sewerage companies of England and Wales led to a significant increase in output prices. Yet, there are counter-examples: Okten and Arin (2006) show that the privatization of cement plants in Turkey led to a significant decline of input prices for the construction industry.[8] Hence, it is questionable whether privatization is really an effective means of bringing down inflation rates. All in all, the inflation rate seems to be less suitable than GDP growth as a measure of economic problem pressure for both theoretical and empirical reasons.

The Stage of Economic Development

No less than nine empirical studies include the level of current or average annual GDP per capita as a control variable in their regressions. It is not immediately apparent why and how the level of GDP should affect privatization. From a comparative perspective, one could presume that 'privatization is driven by economic development, with wealthy and mature countries experiencing the roll-back of the state from economic activity after a stage when it played a crucial role in capital accumulation and investment in infrastructure' (Bortolotti et al. 2003: 320).

Testing this assertion would require a mixed sample of countries, some of which already have passed the invisible threshold between economically premature and mature. Economic laggards should exhibit a negative relationship between GDP and privatization revenues, while the already advanced countries should exhibit a strictly positive relationship. Unfortunately, most of the studies including GDP levels use relatively homogenous samples consisting of OECD, EU, or developing countries. Bortolotti et al. (2001, 2003) utilize relatively large mixed samples and find in one regression that rich GDP countries are more likely to privatize. Note, however, that their regression models are not appropriate to detect a nonlinear relationship between GDP and privatization. Unfortunately, none of the studies explicitly tries to assess the 'tipping point' suggested by Bortolotti et al. (2003) or to check for nonlinearities.

---

[8] Further empirical studies are listed in the survey by Megginson and Netter (2001).

Actor Preferences

In this section, we focus on the influence of actor preferences on privatization. In order to explore the role of *political partisanship* for privatization, we first discuss the theoretical and empirical contributions of Partisan Theory (Hibbs, 1975). Thereafter, we consider the influence of *interest groups*, namely labour unions and employers' associations, on the timing and depth of privatization.

Political Partisanship

Partisan Theory (hereinafter referred to as PT) was developed by Hibbs in the 1970s (Hibbs 1975, 1977, 1986; for a survey see Hibbs 1992). It rests on the stylized fact that left-wing parties have their constituencies in the working class whose members earn their living mostly from low-skilled labour and are exposed to greater risks of job loss. Hence, the working class has a great interest in keeping macro-economic fluctuations low as it has to bear the major burden of economic downturn via rising unemployment. By contrast, right-wing parties have their constituencies in the middle and upper classes, their members owning the better part of private financial capital and occupying more secure jobs. Hence supporters of right-wing parties have a greater interest in low inflation rates than left-wing party supporters. In short, the working class prefer a different point on the Phillips curve[9] than the middle and upper classes. Partisan theory holds that parties primarily enact policies that are consistent with the preferences of their core constituencies. Partisan preferences therefore should be reflected in different macro-economic policies and outcomes under left-wing and right-wing governments (Hibbs 1992: 362–4). In this respect, PT differs considerably from political business cycle theory (PBCT) in the tradition of Nordhaus (1975), Rogoff and Sibert (1988), and Rogoff (1990) implying that all parties will implement the same expansionary policies before elections. Accordingly, ideological party differences that form the backbone of PT are expected to vanish in PBCT models.[10]

Just having seen the light of the day, PT (like Nordhaus' 1975, original adaptive PBCT) was challenged by the rational expectations revolution in

---

[9] The term Phillips curve refers to the empirical observation that times of high inflation were associated with low unemployment and vice versa until the stagflation crisis in the 1970s. The trade off was discovered by Phillips (1958) for the United Kingdom and later replicated for the U.S. (Samuelson and Solow, 1960) and many other industrialized countries. Mortensen (1970) and others made significant contributions to the integration of the Phillips curve into macro-economic modelling. The failure of the classical Phillips curve to correctly predict the relationship between inflation and unemployment after the stagflation crisis was predicted by Friedman (1968) and Phelps (1968), who put into question that wage setters would permanently misconceive the inflation rate.

[10] A model combining elements of PT and PBCT was proposed by Frey and Schneider (1978a, 1978b).

macro-economics, which showed that the classical Phillips curve trade off could only be exploited by unanticipated demand policy (Lucas 1973; Sargent and Wallace 1975). The theory of nominal rigidities (Fischer 1977; Taylor 1980), however, made a revival of PT possible. In the presence of long-term or staggered wage setting, output and employment could be affected by properly timed demand policy. This idea was taken up by Alesina (1987) in a two-party rational expectations model ('Rational Partisan Theory'). The model predicts that partisan effects should always become visible in the period after an election, where uncertainty about the orientation of the new government is resolved. Hence, one should observe recessions and low inflation rates at the beginning of right-wing governments and high employment accompanied by inflation at the beginning of left-wing governments. In the course of the term in office, output and unemployment equalize under both types of government, while inflation remains higher during a left-wing government (for further details and later model modifications see Alesina and Rosenthal 1995; Alesina et al. 1997).

The issue whether and how parties affect short-term macro-economic performance is not settled from an empirical point of view although PT seems to outperform PBCT (Franzese 2002). Hibbs (1978) and Alesina et al. (1997) find strong support for PT in OECD countries (for recent literature surveys see, e.g. Hibbs 2006 and Potrafke 2012). Investigating a long panel of OECD countries Potrafke (2012: 155) concludes that political cycles are more likely to occur in two-party systems, where 'voters can directly punish or reward political parties for governmental performance'. In two-party systems growth is boosted before elections by right-wing governments and after elections by left-wing governments.

PT has also been applied to privatization policy, where the divergent national privatization paths after the stagflation crisis could possibly be traced back to the partisan orientation of the cabinet. Boix (1997: 478) argues that conservative and centre-right parties, who were blamed for having had the wrong economic answers to the Great Depression and, therefore, of having been responsible for high unemployment, agreed to Keynesian demand management and public intervention in the so-called 'post-war consensus' (Hall 1986) as long as this arrangement was able to sustain economic growth and full employment. As soon as this policy approach failed to deliver the promised goals, however, the non-socialist parties switched back to their market-friendly and non-interventionist original positions.

Biais and Perotti (2002) were the first to formalize the idea that targeted privatization could be used by right-wing parties as a strategic policy to retain power ('Machiavellian Privatization'). In their bipartisan model, the right-wing party gains the support of the relatively poor median-class voters, who would naturally vote for the left-wing party serving their redistribution preferences, by underpricing the shares of the SOEs. In the extreme case, SOEs are privatized by voucher or mass privatization (Boycko et al. 1994). To the extent that their shareholdings increase, the median-class voters become more and more averse to left-wing economic policies that would decrease the value of their investments. Schmidt (2000) shows theoretically that mass privatizations motivate the median voter to vote for less income distribution. Megginson et al. (2004) report empirical evidence that right-wing governments actually underprice shares and target more individual investors when privatizing SOEs, and that underpricing increases income inequality (see also Perotti 2013).

A great number of papers investigate PT empirically in the field of privatization. Boix (1997) includes an index of socialist control of the government in his regression models. The index measures the proportion of socialist and communist cabinet portfolios within a government. As hypothesized, the respective coefficients are significant and negative. A purely non-socialist government exhibits a probability to privatize of about 50 per cent, while purely socialist governments are predicted not to privatize at all. In terms of privatization revenues this difference amounts to about 2.7 per cent of GDP. In addition, he employs a self-compiled index of government ideology assuming values between 1 (pro-public ownership) and 20 (anti-public ownership). This government ideology index basically produces the same result. An anti-public ownership attitude of the government makes privatizations more likely and increases privatization revenues. Other indicators of political partisanship, such as the proportion of centrist ministers in cabinet and the partisan affiliation of the minister of finance, turn out to be insignificant. In sum, Boix (1997: 495) concludes for the 1980s that '[r]ight-wing cabinets... pushed through sizable privatization packages. By contrast, left-wing governments... kept intact and, in some cases, expanded the public business sector'.

Without mentioning Boix's (1997) previous work, Bortolotti et al. (2001, 2003) also highlight the importance of a government's ideological position for analysing privatization. Their test of partisan theory is implemented by means of a 'right' dummy variable, assuming a value of one if the majority of privatizations happen under a democratic conservative government and zero otherwise. They find that conservative governments exhibit a higher privatization propensity and privatize relatively more firms. However, parties do not differ in terms of revenues. Furthermore, conservative governments prefer privatizations via public offerings over direct sales, adding support to the hypothesis that they aim at benefiting their constituencies. By contrast, Meseguer (2004: 317) reports left-wing governments to be more likely to launch privatization programmes and attributes this unexpected result to a wide-spread 'consensus across the ideological spectrum... concerning modernisation via downsizing the state-owned sector'.

Schneider et al. (2005) find no evidence for partisan politics playing a role in infrastructure service sector privatization using pooled times-series regression. When controlling for time by running separate regressions for each year, they find partisan theory only confirmed for the 1980s. After then, the 'motto became everyone privatizes' (Schneider et al. 2005: 720). By contrast, Belke et al. (2007) report a strong positive correlation between the share of right-party portfolios and privatization revenues. Under a purely conservative government annual privatization revenues would increase by about 0.4–0.5 per cent of GDP. Zohlnhöfer et al. (2008) cannot find partisan effects in their EU sample, except in a cross-section for the period of 1998–2000. In contrast, the cabinet share of bourgeois parties turns out to be highly significant in their OECD sample. Bortolotti and Pinotti (2008) show that government ideology has a significant effect on the timing of privatization. As suggested by partisan theory, right-wing governments start privatization programmes earlier. Similarly, Schuster et al. (2013) detect that right-wing governments speed up privatization programmes, but only in terms of obtaining revenues and not in terms of reducing public employment.

Schneider and Häge (2008) find a strong negative correlation between the cabinet share of left parties and public infrastructure privatization. Fink (2011), by contrast, cannot find an impeding impact of left-wing governments on the decision to privatize the telecom sector after controlling for spatial diffusion of privatization policies. Even though all early telecom privatizations, except in Spain, were carried out by non-leftist governments, he argues that partisan preferences were influential only in the 1980s. Thereafter privatization became accepted as more and more governments emulated the privatization policies adopted elsewhere. Schmitt's (2011) analysis of policy diffusion in the telecom sector reveals no impact of the cabinet share of left-wing parties. Investigating the privatization of three infrastructure sectors, namely postal services, telecom, and railways, Schmitt and Obinger (2011) obtain the same finding. Roberts and Saeed (2012) find neither more privatization deals nor higher revenues in years when right-wing governments are in office. Likewise, the cabinet seat share of leftist parties turns out to be insignificant when regressed on an index of public entrepreneurship in a spatial regression framework (Schmitt 2014a). She concludes: '[T]he results show that the pressure to move in line with economically related countries towards more market and less state intervention is the same for all parties independent of their party affiliation' (Schmitt 2014a: 629).

It is a bit surprising that only one study explicitly controls for the impact of elections on privatization programmes as suggested by rational PT. Bortolotti et al. (2003) report that governments generally sell significantly less stakes in election years than in non-election years. Roberts and Saeed (2012), however, do use the number of a government's years in office as a covariate in their regressions, although the variable turns out to be insignificant.

Overall, the hypothesis that political partisanship explains cross-national differences in the timing and extent of privatization is generally supported by the empirical literature. This proposition comes with a strong qualification, however. In terms of privatization, several studies suggest that partisan differences have disappeared over the years. Zohlnhöfer et al. (2008), for example, argue that the alignment process was particularly strong in the EU with its single-market programme. Despite major ideological differences in party platforms between left and bourgeois parties with regard to privatization and nationalization (cf. Budge et al. 2001), they find that 'partisan differences disappear if governments are exposed to substantial economic problem pressure' (Zohlnhöfer et al. 2008: 115). Hence, left parties privatize even if they are not convinced of privatization as a tool for increasing macro-economic efficiency. This view finds support in Schmitt's (2014a) spatial analysis.

Interest Groups

The notion that the power resources of interest groups such as unions are important in understanding public policy outcomes has featured prominently in macro-sociology and political science for decades (Korpi 1983). As its core, power resource theory holds that employers and employees have antagonistic interests with the resulting conflict decided by their respective power resources. Since the crucial power resource of the labour movement is its size and the right to vote, union density and left seats in parliament or government are key indicators for measuring the influence of the labour movement on public policy. Economists also regard interest groups as relevant actors for explaining economic performance and public policy outcomes (Olson 1982). Mueller and Murrel (1986), for example, find for a set of OECD countries a positive relationship between the 'size of government' and the number of officially registered economic interest groups such as chambers of commerce and labour unions.

While unions are mostly seen as reluctant to privatization, the underlying causal mechanisms are seldom made explicit. The resistance-to-change literature has a long tradition in analysing the psychological mechanisms that lead employees to resist organizational change and gives advice on how to manage it (Coch and French 1948; Piderit 2000). Privatization is a major organizational change that involves ex-ante uncertainty for personnel in terms of privatization outcomes such as job losses, wage inequality, and loss of power. Hence labour unions can be expected to fight privatization with all available means. A similar argument is made by Fernandez and Rodrik (1991), who argued that efficiency-enhancing but inequality-increasing reforms that involve ex-ante uncertainty about the distribution of gains and losses are likely to be rejected even if the reform outcome would be preferred by a majority from an ex-post perspective. The resulting status-quo bias prevents policy makers from adopting reforms like privatization that are considered to be efficiency-enhancing.[11]

The empirical evidence concerning the influence of unions on privatization is at best mixed. With the exception of Schmitt and Obinger (2011), all studies employ an index of strike activity in terms of working days lost due to industrial conflict. Strike activity serves as a proxy variable for labour unions' distaste for privatization, for union density, and for their militancy. Belke et al. (2007) and Zohlnhöfer et al. (2008) report strike activities to have a negative impact on privatization revenues. Bortolotti and Pinotti (2008) cannot find evidence of a delay in privatization due to labour unions' resistance. According to Schuster et al. (2013) strike activity does not affect changes in the stock of SOEs in terms of privatized revenues and employment. Schmitt and Obinger (2011), who investigate the influence of labour union density on privatization intensity in public utilities sectors, also report insignificant coefficients.

To our knowledge, the influence of employers' associations on privatization has not so far been investigated empirically. In a manner similar to Obinger and Zohlnhöfer (2005), Belke et al. (2007) argue that employers' associations might be in favour of privatizing public utilities like telecom, electricity, and transport—aspiring to lower charges stemming from the expected efficiency gains. Moreover, they might also wish to become investors in the former SOEs. Belke et al. (2007: 221) conclude, however, that employers due to their diverging interests 'are unlikely to express their strong interest in favour of privatization policies'.

---

[11] There have been several attempts to assess the distributional consequences of privatization in terms of wage and employment changes, which are labour unions' main concern. Surveying twenty-two empirical privatization studies from non-transition economies, Megginson and Netter (2001: 356–66) conclude that there is 'no standard outcome' for the impact of privatization on employment levels, neither at the firm nor at the sector levels. Employment reductions are likely to occur if productivity gains are not accompanied by increasing sales. Examining the experiences of several mixed economies, the World Bank concludes in a similar vein that large-scale labour force reductions take place first and foremost in poorly managed SOEs that are no match for competition (Kikeri 1998). Brown et al. (2010) find no job losses due to privatization in transition economies. Foreign ownership increases employment due to a massive scale effect, exceeding the productivity effect by far. Interestingly, the World Bank judges that labour union influence decreases after privatization (Kikeri 1998). Birdsall and Nellis (2003) suggest that privatization is responsible for increasing wage differentials between skilled and unskilled labour. Schmitt (2014b) shows that privatization leads to a reduction in the number of employees in the public utility sectors. However, the downsizing takes place before material privatization.

Institutions

In this section, we address the role of institutions and their interactions with political actors in the timing and depth of privatization programmes. Institutions determine the number of actors involved in policy making, their interactions, and their room to manoeuvre. The first subsection investigates the type of democracy (Lijphart 2012), whereas the next subsection is dedicated to veto player theory (Tsebelis 2002) and its potential contribution to the explanation of cross-country variation in privatization policies. Here, we focus on the number, partisan orientation, and internal coherence of institutional and partisan veto players. The law and finance literature suggests that a country's legal origin has a considerable impact on the development of financial markets due to different capacities of legal systems to adapt to new economic requirements (Beck et al. 2003). The third subsection is therefore concerned with the relationship between legal origin, financial markets, and privatization. Capital market development, which is seen both as an essential institutional prerequisite and a goal of privatization, is addressed in the fourth subsection. Next, we discuss constitutional provisions as a possible determinant of privatization intensity (Schmitt and Obinger 2011). Finally, privatization might be path-dependent and shaped by the policy legacy of the past as new governments inherit the policies of their predecessors. In the final subsection, we therefore turn to the initial size of the public sector.

Consensus vs. Majoritarian Democracy

A key institutional characteristic distinguishing majoritarian from consensus democracies is the electoral system. The electoral system defines how votes are counted and aggregated. Plurality voting promotes two-party systems and one-party governments. The so-called Westminster or majoritarian model of democracy thus enables governments to enforce their policy programmes more easily. Proportional representation is associated with multi-party systems, coalition governments, and a more balanced power relationship between executive and legislative. In a nutshell, the consensus model of democracy 'tries to limit, divide, separate, and share power in a variety of ways' (Lijphart 1991: 73). The capacity of coalition governments to implement privatization policies is expected to be altered in two ways (Boix 1997). Firstly, coalition governments likely contain the median party (Laver and Schofield 1990). The inclusion of the median party is assumed to have a moderating effect on policy programmes (Fiorina 1996; also see Alesina and Rosenthal 1995, 1996). Secondly, reforms like privatization programmes have distributional consequences that hit the constituencies of the coalition parties in different ways. Multi-party governments therefore involve troublesome negotiations among the coalition partners about the allocation of reform burdens. A consequence of this 'war of attrition' (Alesina and Drazen 1991; Spolaore 2004) is that even reforms that are expected to increase efficiency will either be carried out incrementally or be subject to procrastination ('gridlock effect'). Hence, radical privatization (or nationalization) programmes have been hypothesized to be less likely with proportional representation and coalition governments than with majority vote and one-party governments.

The only empirical study directly controlling for the electoral system was published by Bortolotti and Pinotti (2008). They use Gallagher's (1991) measure of the disproportionality of the electoral system, a continuous index number that ranges from 0 under perfect proportional representation to a value that equals the share of votes obtained by the defeated candidate in a presidential election, that is, the most extreme majoritarian election system. Boix (1997), Bortolotti and Pinotti (2008), and Zohlnhöfer et al. (2008) examine the impact of government fragmentation on privatization programmes by means of various indices. Boix (1997) employs Rae's (1968) Government Fragmentation Index ranging from 0 for one-party governments to 1 for extreme fragmentation. Bortolotti and Pinotti (2008) use the Effective Number of Parties introduced by Laakso and Taagepera (1979), which is an application of the Herfindahl index of political power concentration based on the number of seats held by the different parties in parliament. Zohlnhöfer et al. (2008) use a government fragmentation index, too. A plain dummy variable for majority governments is applied by Boix (1997). Zohlnhöfer et al. (2008) measure the time a minority government held office as a percentage of the relevant period of observation.

The empirical evidence concerning the impact of government structures on the timing and depth of privatization programmes is mixed. For the 1980s, Boix (1997) finds strong support for the hypothesis that majority governments are more likely to start a privatization programme and also privatize more in terms of revenues. Likewise, Bortolotti and Pinotti (2008) report that privatizations are delayed by the consensus model of democracy with its larger number of parties, lower concentration of power, and a more relentless 'war of attrition'. In contrast, Zohlnhöfer et al. (2008) find no impact of government fragmentation on privatization proceeds in OECD countries. Surprisingly, for their EU sample, they even find that minority governments privatize more than majority governments. The puzzle is solved when taking into account the findings noted above that privatization activities seem to have become uncoupled from political partisanship in the 1990s. Hence, it would appear that it has become much easier even for fragmented or minority governments to gain political support for new privatization programmes.

Veto Players

A status-quo bias in policy making might also be caused by veto players (Henisz 2000; Tsebelis 2002). Generally speaking, 'veto players are individual or collective actors whose agreement is necessary for a change of the status quo. It follows that a change in the status quo requires a unanimous decision of all veto players' (Tsebelis 2002: 36). Veto player theory (VPT) distinguishes between institutional veto players that are created by the constitution (e.g. the President and the Senate) and partisan veto players that are generated by the political game (e.g. the parties forming a coalition). Hence, VPT essentially combines an actor-centred model like Partisan Theory with institutional restrictions.

VPT holds that the timing and depth of privatization programmes depends on the number of veto players, the magnitude of ideological differences between different veto players, and the internal cohesion of each collective veto player (which in turn is positively related to its number of members, Tsebelis 2002: 74). Each of these factors is assumed to shrink the 'winset', that is, the policy space that could replace the status quo. In order to test VPT, a set of indices aggregating number, ideological differences, and cohesion has been developed. Henisz compiled the Political Constraints Index (POLCON). It ranges from 0 (least constrained) to 1 (most constrained) and takes into account the number of independent branches of government with veto power over policy reform as well as the party composition of the executive and legislative bodies. POLCON is applied by Henisz et al. (2005), Schneider et al. (2005), and Fink (2011). Belke et al. (2007) rely on a veto player index developed by Keefer (2002) and first applied by Keefer and Stasavage (2003). Schneider and Häge (2008) prefer Schmidt's (1996) Index of Institutional Constraints over the VPT, because they expect it to be more suitable for the field of infrastructure liberalization and privatization than its competitor. Schmitt (2011) and Schmitt and Obinger (2011) include the Index of Institutional Constraints proposed by Huber et al. (1993) using Armingeon's Comparative Political Data Set (Armingeon et al. 2011) as a control variable in their analyses. It comprises five indicators: federalism, presidentialism, electoral system, bicameralism, and referenda. Zohlnhöfer et al. (2008) investigate the impact of bicameralism, federalism, and constitutional rigidity using data compiled by Lijphart (1999).

Moreover, unidimensional indicators related to federalism and corporatism have been utilized in empirical inquiries. Federalism is seen as an impediment to privatization due to the high number of veto players enshrined in federal systems (Belke et al. 2007; Bortolotti and Pinotti 2008). Though usually at an informal level, corporatist systems of interest mediation (as opposed to pluralist systems) incorporate the peak associations of labour and capital into political decision making (Schmitter and Lehmbruch 1979). Since unions are usually affiliated with the left and unions typically oppose privatizations, corporatism is expected to impede privatizations because of the informal veto power of trade unions in the negotiation process. Schneider and Häge (2008) and Schmitt and Obinger (2011) include Siaroff's (1999) Corporatism Index into their regressions in order to test the corporatism hypothesis.

Only three of the aforementioned studies come up with statistically significant negative coefficients for the multidimensional indices. Schneider et al. (2005) find, as expected, state ownership to increase with rising veto points, though only in the electricity sector. POLCON proves to be insignificant in all sectors. Hence, they conclude that institutional factors cannot sufficiently explain country differences with regard to privatization. It might be beneficial, however, to use sector-specific disaggregated privatization data. Belke et al. (2007: 236) conclude analogously that 'institutional factors display a less systematic effect than economic and political variables'. Zohlnhöfer et al. (2008) report negative coefficients of their institutional constraints index for both the EU and the OECD sample. Both studies investigating the corporatism hypothesis reject it (Schneider and Häge 2008; Schmitt and Obinger 2011). Bortolotti and Pinotti's (2008) study reveals a significant delay of privatization programmes in federal countries; yet, the degree of federalism is irrelevant for privatization revenues (Belke et al. 2007). In summary, we conclude that the empirical base of the hypothesis that institutional constraints in terms of veto players have played a role for the timing and depth of privatization programmes is not overwhelming.

Legal Origin

Cross-country variation of privatization activities has also been attributed to a country's legal system. Bortolotti et al. (2003: 309) emphasize the 'well documented fact that civil law countries—particularly with the French civil law tradition—have a larger SOE sector with respect to common law countries'. La Porta et al. (1998) report an average size of the SOE sector in terms of value added of 15 per cent for French civil law countries as compared to 11 per cent for common law countries. German civil law countries are closer to common law countries (12 per cent). The governments of French civil law countries also exhibit a generally more interventionist orientation and a tendency to operate their SOEs inefficiently (La Porta and Lopez-de-Silanes 1999; La Porta et al. 2002).

The link between the legal system and privatization is established by the financial market. Since privatization programmes come along with capital market development, different regulations in the legal system related to investors, property rights, and financial markets might have different repercussions on the practicability and success of privatization programmes (the 'political' channel). Moreover, it has been hypothesized that legal systems differ in their ability to adapt to changing economic circumstances (the 'adaptability' channel). Beck et al. (2003), who also provide a careful survey of the law and finance literature, infer that (i) civil law systems generally tend to create institutions that augment state power and hinder financial market development and (ii) that French legal origin countries have a much lower adaptability than British common law and German civil law countries. Examining a sample of up to 115 countries with French, German, and Scandinavian civil and British common law traditions, they find a lower adaptability of French civil law systems. Hence, one should expect French civil law countries to privatize later and less than other civil law countries as well as countries with a common law tradition.

A tendency of French and German civil law countries to privatize less than common law countries is actually reported by Bortolotti et al. (2001, 2003). Yet, the hypothesis that the lower adaptability of civil law as compared to common law systems hinders privatization is only supported by half of their regressions. Brune et al. (2004), on the contrary, find no differences between British and French legal heritage countries. Hence, we put on record that the evidence related to the impact of legal origin on privatization is inconsistent.

Capital Market Development

It has been convincingly argued in the literature that developed capital markets constitute a necessary condition for the success of privatization programmes in terms of their ability to generate revenue (Bortolotti et al. 2003). According to Levine (1997), financial markets reduce information asymmetries and transactions costs. For instance, Holmström and Tirole (1993) show that stock prices contain information about managerial performance that cannot be extracted from firms' current or future profits. Concentrated ownership reduces liquidity and limits the amount of information reflected in stock prices. 'Where financial markets are well developed and efficient, governments should privatise more, as there is less risk of shareholders being expropriated by managers' (Bortolotti et al. 2001: 115).

Most of the studies investigating the role of capital market development find a significant impact both on privatization timing and privatization depth in terms of revenues. From this point of view, capital market development (usually measured in terms of liquidity) contributes to explaining differences in national privatization trajectories. However, one could as well argue the other way round that privatization is a vehicle for developing capital markets. This view is strongly supported by international data on capital market development (see Boutchkova and Megginson 2000; Megginson et al. 2004).

Hence, if liquidity on the one hand affects the success of privatization and privatization increases liquidity on the other, one runs into an endogeneity problem when using standard regression techniques. Therefore, it would be best to leave the question open of whether capital market development has actually *causally* determined privatization paths.

Constitutional Provisions

Constitutional provisions can limit the scope of privatization programmes and retard privatization processes because constitutional amendments require greater political majorities than ordinary legislation. Briefly reviewing the legal literature on the privatization of SOEs, Schmitt and Obinger (2011) discuss several constitutional provisions related to public utilities which might hinder privatization. For example, a constitutional provision related to a (typically privileged) public service might retard privatizations because it necessitates a transformation of the employment contracts of SOE personnel. A country's constitution might also define social rights, state duties, or state principles which cannot easily be transferred from the public to the private sector.[12] Furthermore, the constitution can explicitly allocate the provision (but not necessarily the production) of public goods and services to the government. It can even stipulate a privatization ban. In such cases, alternatives like private–public partnership (Hodge et al. 2010) might be politically more feasible than reaching a broad political consensus on the privatization of such goods and services.

Schmitt and Obinger (2011) and Schmitt (2014a) are the first and only authors to explicitly check for the role of constitutional provisions in national privatization activities. Schmitt and Obinger (2011) employ a six-dimensional index of constitutional barriers to privatization, including public services, social rights, state duties, regulations, and state principles. The index borrows from the legal-origin literature by accounting for the fact that common law countries generally exhibit a higher degree of adaptability. Empirically, they investigate the privatization activities of twenty-one OECD countries in the telecom, postal, and railways sectors. The authors find that constitutional regulations related to these public utility sectors are more pronounced in southern European and German-speaking countries than in English-speaking countries. Differences in the index explain cross-country variation in privatization intensities in the telecom and railways sectors but not in the postal sector. The negative finding for the postal sector is attributed to the hitherto

---

[12] For example, Schuster (2013) shows that, despite universal service obligations, the privatization of postal services leads to a significant decrease of service quality in OECD countries.

relatively low level of privatization activities in the postal sector. Schmitt (2014a) confirms these results using different data and a spatial econometric framework.

The Initial Size of the SOE Sector

Governments can only privatize firms that previously have been in public hands (Zohlnhöfer et al. 2008). Quite naturally, even the greatest data set is delimited by a starting year. Low privatization revenues (standardized by GDP) in the observation period might result from a government's reluctance to sell off the 'family silver' or simply from a low starting value of public ownership. A low starting value could in turn mean that the privatization wave has already coasted to a standstill or that state ownership never played a major role in the respective country. A well-executed econometric study on the determinants of privatization therefore has to carefully control for the initial size of the SOE sector. Empirical studies that exclude countries from the sample due to low privatization revenues or low initial levels of public ownership must somehow deal with sample selection bias, whereas studies including countries with zero observed values on the endogenous variable must deal with data censoring (Heckman 1979). In fact, such studies are rather the exception than the rule in the empirical privatization literature.[13]

First of all, a good indicator of public ownership, ideally a stock figure, has to be found. Several different indicators have been used in the literature. Bortolotti et al. (2001) control for the size of the SOE sector in the year before a country's first privatization by a World Bank (1995) index containing the share of SOE assets over GDP, the share of SOEs in employment, and the share of SOE investment in gross domestic investment. The indicator 'Government Enterprises and Public Sector Investment as a Share of the Economy' by Gwartney and his co-authors (Gwartney et al. 1996; Gwartney and Lawson 2000) is employed by two inquiries (Brune et al. 2004; Zohlnhöfer et al. 2008). Measuring the general extent of state regulation in the economy, the Economic Freedom Index (Gwartney and Lawson 2000, 2004) is utilized by Belke et al. (2007), Zohlnhöfer et al. (2008), and Roberts and Saeed (2012), yet in different ways. Zohlnhöfer et al. (2008) rely on the index value at the

---

[13] For example, Schuster et al. (2013), who left out the U.S. due to data restrictions on the endogenous variable, noted that sample selection might lead to upward-biased slope coefficients and overestimated significance of explanatory variables (that would absorb omitted variables from the neglected selection equation). Bortolotti et al. (2003: 325) acknowledged the censoring problem and advised their readers to interpret their estimates in a non-causal manner as conditional expectations. In contrast, Brune et al. (2004) explicitly controlled for censoring by applying tobit regression analysis.

beginning of their observation period in 1990, whereas Belke et al. (2007) and Roberts and Saeed (2012) plug current values into their panel regressions—a choice which might make some readers wonder about endogeneity issues. In their duration analysis, Bortolotti and Pinotti (2008) use the 1977 values of an averaged index of public ownership across different sectors of economic activity provided by the OECD (Conway and Nicoletti 2006).

Table 3.1 shows that among those studies controlling for state ownership or more generally for the degree of economic freedom at the beginning of privatization the results are mixed. Bortolotti et al. (2001) and Bortolotti and Pinotti (2008) do not find a significant impact of the legacy of the past on several privatization measures and timing. Brune et al. (2004) and Zohlnhöfer et al. (2008) report significant regression coefficients exhibiting the expected sign (positive for public ownership and negative for economic freedom). Belke et al.'s (2007) surprising result that higher economic freedom is correlated with more privatization might indeed be attributed to a simultaneity problem. Altogether, our reading of the literature suggests that the initial size of the public sector has a slight positive impact on privatization activities. However, irrespective of its sign and significance, providing some starting value for public involvement is clearly a must-have in regression models. Note that Schmitt (2011), Schuster et al. (2013), Schmitt and Obinger (2011), and Schmitt (2014a) avoid the problem of finding a starting value by employing stock indices of public entrepreneurship.

International Influences

As already noted in Chapter 2, globalization is characterized by increased international economic integration due to technical progress, decreasing transport costs, and international trade liberalization (Bordo et al. 1999). For a single country, the phenomenon manifests itself as a permanent shock. Globalization shock waves, however, spread out over uneven territories. Even though almost all countries have become more integrated into the world economy since the beginning of privatization programmes in the 1980s, their levels of *economic integration* and, in consequence, the relative importance of globalization pressures differed substantially. The degree of economic integration might therefore help to explain cross-national variation in privatization timing and depth (Schneider and Häge 2008). Apart from economic integration, *Europeanization* has been considered as one of the main international influences on national privatization policies. Europeanization is addressed in a second subsection. In the final subsection, we turn to policy diffusion. The empirical investigation of the phenomenon requires specific econometric regression methods.

Economic Integration

Investigating the impact of economic integration on privatization activities also provides a specific test of two competing hypotheses on a country's reaction to globalization, namely the efficiency hypothesis and the compensation hypothesis. According to the former, globalization pressures might disempower national governments and force them into austerity, deregulation, and privatization in order to limber up their economies for global competition (Strange 1996). In contrast, the compensation thesis argues that public spending and state intervention increase with the objective of providing income guarantees and automatic stabilizers against the risks and instabilities of globalization and market fluctuations (Garret 1998; Rodrik 1998). In this respect, the SOE sector could constitute an ideal hideaway for the socially disadvantaged and losers of globalization.

Schneider et al. (2005) measure economic integration by three indicators, each representing a different dimension of economic openness: firstly, the usual measure of trade openness, i.e. the sum of exports and imports as a percentage of GDP; secondly, financial openness in terms of a country's regulation of capital flows (Quinn 1997); and, thirdly, inward foreign direct investment (FDI). The trade openness indicator is also employed by Brune et al. (2004), Meseguer (2004), Belke et al. (2007), Schneider and Häge (2008), Schmitt (2011), Schuster et al. (2013), and Schmitt (2014a). Except for Belke et al. (2007), none of the studies investigating OECD countries is able to reject the null hypothesis that trade openness does not affect privatization. Moreover, in some of the robustness checks provided by Belke et al. (2007), the impact of trade openness vanishes.

Financial openness is also investigated by Zohlnhöfer et al. (2008) and Schneider and Häge (2008). The regression results are even more to the disadvantage of the efficiency hypothesis. The only important exception is Schneider et al. (2005), who find a strong negative impact of openness related to capital flows on state ownership in infrastructure sectors. Since all other variables turn out to be insignificant, they conclude that 'the opening of the economy to international capital flows is the sole driving force behind privatization' (p. 719). Quite astonishingly, one of the authors reports the reverse effect (though the coefficients are insignificant) in a later inquiry of public infrastructure privatization (Schneider and Häge 2008). A qualitative comparison of both studies reveals that Schneider et al. (2005) use a larger sample and pooled time-series data, while Schneider and Häge (2008) rely on a smaller sample and cross-section regressions. Finally, inward FDI fails to reach significance in both studies paying attention to it (Schneider et al. 2005; Zohlnhöfer et al. 2008).

On the basis of literature reviewed in this section, we conclude that the degree of economic integration only partially explains cross-country differences in privatization timing and depth. In particular, financial openness seems to influence infrastructure privatization. With regard to the compensation and the efficiency hypotheses, we can neither testify systematic negative nor positive effects of the degree of economic integration on privatization. Governments apparently privatize more or less independently of the national level of international economic integration, suggesting that globalization might be a common trigger for privatization, but does not play an outstanding role in shaping cross-national differences.

Europeanization

The phenomenon of Europeanization is multifaceted (Olsen 2002). Europeanization can be regarded as a regional form of globalization (Verdier and Breen 2001), thus increasing competitive pressure among member states. In addition, member states have to transpose the policies adopted at the European level. Since market building and liberalization have been at the top of the agenda of European policy makers in recent decades, Europeanization, like globalization, can be seen as a stimulus for national governments to privatize public enterprises with a view to improving economic efficiency. Since EU member states are exposed to both globalization and common European policies, reform pressure might be more severe inside than outside the EU. A milestone of European integration was the formation of the Single European Market. From the 1980s onwards, the European Commission regarded the liberalization and deregulation of network-based industries and public services as important prerequisites for achieving this goal (Scharpf 1999). So-called greenbooks and directives set up the framework for the liberalization and privatization of the telecommunications sector (COM/87/290) and the postal sector (COM/91/476). In contrast to these sectors, the liberalization of the railways sector was tackled late and has made relatively little progress (see Schmitt 2014a; Knill and Lehmkuhl 2007). By means of two directives enacted in 1996 and 2003, the EU required its member states to unbundle their electricity industries, to gradually open their markets, and to set up independent regulatory authorities. However, European countries' electricity markets are still far away from being united (Jamasb and Pollitt 2005).

Meseguer (2004) does not find an impact of EU membership on the likelihood of launching privatizations. Investigating a sample of twenty OECD countries, Schneider and Häge (2008) observe EU member states to significantly outperform other countries in their privatization efforts with regard to public infrastructures. The authors conclude that 'Europeanization promoted infrastructure privatization' (p. 16). Likewise, Fink (2011) finds EU membership to have significantly accelerated national governments' decisions to privatize the telecommunications sector. By contrast, Schmitt (2011: 113) concludes that 'the privatization of telecommunications services was a global trend and not primarily triggered by the European Union'. Schmitt and Obinger (2011) find a significant negative impact of Europeanization on privatization intensity in the railways sector. No impact is found for the postal sector. Schuster et al. (2013) cannot find evidence of an impact of EU membership or of EU accession on the extent of state ownership. Schmitt (2013) demonstrates that the influence of European integration on privatization differs across sectors. She finds that privatization in the telecommunications sector is a worldwide policy fashion while privatization in the postal sector is pushed by European integration. In contrast, in the railways sector, certain EU regulations have decelerated the privatization of national railway service providers.

Spatial Diffusion

Emphasizing that game theoretic approaches to politics rest upon the very idea that political actors are engaged in strategic behaviour, Gilardi (2010: 650) recently tagged interdependence as a 'defining feature of politics'. Ross and Homer (1976) thoroughly summarized the problems caused by common shocks and interdependencies for cross-national research. The main challenge for international comparative research—known as 'Galton's Problem'—is that a particular policy (e.g. privatization) can be attributed to explanatory factors at the within-country level or to policy diffusion, that is, the choices made in another country. In the latter case, the observations on the two different countries are not independent because they have a common source in the other country's government. As a result of lacking independence, regression outcomes might be biased in a way similar to the omission of an important exogenous variable. For details on the econometric treatment of (spatial) interdependence, we refer to Franzese and Hays' (2008) excellent essay.

Four channels leading to policy diffusion have been distinguished in the literature: (i) learning, (ii) emulation, (iii) competition, and (iv) coercion (see Elkins and Simmons 2005; Dobbin et al. 2007; Meseguer and Gilardi 2009):

(i) When choosing a policy, national policy makers who are confronted with a certain problem pressure are geared to successful policies approved abroad ('best practices') to reduce the uncertainty in terms of the consequences and outcomes of policies. In consequence, policies may be partly or completely adopted (positive learning) or avoided (negative learning). If, for example, the privatization of SOEs in country A leads to more efficient firms and, in consequence, to better economic performance, country B might learn from this foreign experience and adopt similar policies.

(ii) Closely related to learning and lesson drawing is emulation. While learning generally implies a better understanding of the mechanisms that cause a particular policy outcome, emulation rather refers to the ambitions of policy makers to conform to international policy trends. In the extreme, when a policy adoption is not related to a particular problem pressure or concerns about the efficacy of a particular policy, emulation becomes purely symbolic.

(iii) Competition is based on the strategic interactions of governments. In times of growing international competition, it is likely that governments have to consider other countries' policy choices to realize a competitive advantage or to avoid economic disadvantages vis-à-vis their competitors. For example, privatization might be a strategic choice with a view to improving national economic competitiveness (e.g. via the strengthening of domestic capital markets or by lowering public subsidy payments to industry). Other countries might then be tempted to embark on a similar policy route in order not to fall economically behind.

(iv) The fourth mechanism emphasizes that nation-states are increasingly subject to coercion. Since coercion presupposes an extensive power asymmetry among states, it is rare within developed democracies.

Regrettably, studies explicitly controlling for spatial interdependencies by adequate econometric techniques are rare. Notable exemptions are, for example, Meseguer (2004, 2009), Fink (2011), and Schmitt (2011, 2014a). Acting on the assumption that governments are rational Bayesian learners, Meseguer (2004) tests the hypothesis that countries privatize as a result of learning from their own and other countries' experience. More specifically, she investigates whether the likelihood that a government starts privatization is positively correlated with the expected gain in GDP growth induced by privatization. Meseguer (2004) actually finds a significant positive impact of privatization experiences in 'the rest of the world' (notably from Latin American countries) on privatization activities in the OECD world. According to her, this counter-intuitive result could be explained by the OECD countries' aim to achieve the higher growth rates of the Latin American countries (during the observation period 1980–97) by adopting their privatization policies. Apart from learning, she mainly attributes privatization to emulation or 'herding': in years where many countries privatize, the idiosyncratic likelihood of each country to launch its own privatization programme is elevated.

Fink (2011) argues that domestic factors alone cannot explain the spread of privatization in the telecommunications sector. In fact, he finds strong empirical evidence for policy diffusion: countries observing that other countries belonging to the same welfare state regime in terms of Esping-Andersen's

(1990) famous typology had privatized their telecommunications sector in the previous year are significantly more likely to follow next year. Fink (2011) interprets his results in terms of policy emulation, but one could just as well argue for learning or competition. Perhaps, governments simply aim at avoiding disadvantages for their domestic telecommunications utility in a rapidly growing telecommunications world market. Also note that diffusion is only relevant for the same sector but not for different sectors within a country (which could speak on behalf of learning instead of emulation). Like Fink (2011), Schmitt (2014a) does not find evidence for cross-sector diffusion (between the telecommunications, postal, and railways sectors). Spatial lag coefficients are significant in particular for geographical proximity—for example, Norway closely follows Sweden in privatizing her telecommunications provider 'Telenor'—and among trade partners, where more open economies are 'more receptive to international trends' (Schmitt 2011: 11).

Upshot

We commenced this chapter with an overview of four bodies of theory emphasizing the relevance of economic performance, actor preferences, institutions, and international influences for explaining cross-national variation in privatization pathways. Next, we scrutinized the corresponding macro-quantitative literature focusing on economically advanced countries. Table 3.1 provides an overview of the meta-results obtained from our literature survey. The table lists the determinants with their theoretically expected signs, the number of studies testing the respective hypothesis and classifies the empirical evidence qualitatively. Where it seems appropriate, we additionally comment on the meta-results.

Which conclusions can be drawn from previous quantitative research? When it comes to economic performance, low average long-term GDP growth seems to fuel the timing and depth of privatization, whereas the findings related to current growth point to a weak correlation. Public budget deficits mainly have sparked off privatizations in EU member states with the Maastricht Treaty presumably as a major causal factor. Unemployment turned out significant in one study but the finding might be driven by multicollinearity problems. In a similar vein, inflation was examined only by two studies and the theoretical relationship between inflation and privatization is far from clear. Finally, the extant literature suggests that the level of economic development is unrelated to privatization.

In terms of *actor preferences* the picture obtained is as follows. In the 1980s, partisan differences with regard to privatization were strong. Privatizations were enacted by right-wing governments, while left cabinets as well as coalition governments privatized later and less. In the 1990s, ideological differences still existed, but were less important or even ceased to matter for privatization. The findings related to unions are inconsistent, if anything, unions have hindered privatization.

The evidence for *institutional variables* is mixed. Unequivocal evidence neither exists for the number of veto players nor for a country's legal system origin. Where capital market development is concerned, it is questionable whether the weak positive correlation between financial market development and privatization can be interpreted as a causal relationship because of endogeneity problems: effective financial institutions are important for the success of privatization programmes, while privatizations are often implemented with a view to strengthening financial markets. By contrast, policy-specific constitutional provisions turned out as more convincing explanatory variables. Constitutional provisions such as privatization bans and mandated universal service provision affect the privatization of public utilities. Even though the findings related to the initial public sector size are mixed, one should in any case control for policy legacy of the past in econometric studies.

In terms of *international influences* there is no evidence whatsoever for the compensation thesis, while evidence for the efficiency hypotheses is not really compelling either. Europeanization is important for understanding privatization but its impact seems to vary across sectors. In sectors like telecommunications and postal services, EU influence is more pronounced than in sectors such as railways. Finally, policy diffusion, understood as strategic interactions between governments, plays an important role when explaining privatization.

Arguably, some of the inconsistencies in the extant literature are related to differences in terms of the sample studied, the estimation technique employed, and the time period of analysis. What is more problematic, however, is the fact that most studies only have analysed the timing and extent of material privatization, while formal privatizations were totally neglected. In Chapter 4, we present a new data set that provides information on both dimensions of privatization at the national level before we then turn to our own empirical inquiry in Chapter 5.

4

Mapping the Entrepreneurial State

Data and National Trajectories of Privatization

Having discussed the theoretical foundations of privatization and the state of the existing empirical literature, this chapter is concerned with two issues. First, we introduce our conceptualization of privatization and present our new data set. Next, we take stock of the extent of public entrepreneurship at the beginning of the period under discussion and trace country- and sector-specific privatization and nationalization pathways between 1980 and 2007. A final section summarizes our main descriptive findings.

Privatization: Conceptualization and Data

Before analysing the determinants of privatization, a clear conceptualization of privatization is necessary. When it comes to the privatization of public enterprises, two stages of privatization have to be differentiated: formal and substantial (or material) privatization. Formal privatization is of particular relevance in the public utility sectors. Despite national differences, two substages of formal privatization can be distinguished. The first one refers to the transformation of a *departmental agency* as part of a ministry (e.g. the *Direction Générale des Télécommunication* in France) into a *public corporation* (e.g. France *Télécom*) that is subject to special or public law. While a departmental agency does not have its own legal personality and is subordinated to a ministry, a public corporation is an autonomous public body with its own legal status and a partially commercial structure. Although a law or statute often defines the objectives of a public corporation, such a corporation has more autonomy in day-to-day operations than a departmental agency. The second substage of formal privatization is the change of a public corporation into a *state company* subject to private law in a manner akin to a joint stock company (e.g. British

Political Economy of Privatization in Rich Democracies

Departmental Agency	→	Public Corporation	→	State Company (Public Shares =100%)	→	State Company (Public Shares <100% and >0%)	→	Private Company (Public Shares = 0%)
Formal Privatization		Formal Privatization		Substantial Privatization		Substantial Privatization		

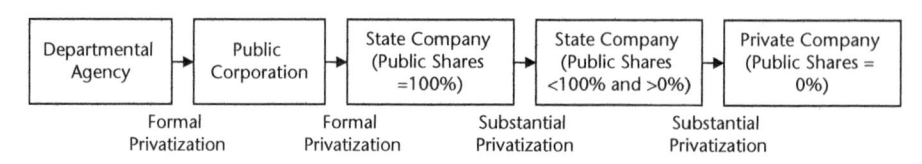

Figure 4.1. Conceptualization of formal and substantial privatization

Telecom plc). A state company is subjected to the same rules and restrictions as private companies, such as a hard budget constraint. In contrast to public corporations or departmental agencies, state companies are only responsible for the well-being of the enterprise itself. The state remains the unique stakeholder. A departmental agency can also be directly transformed into a state company subject to private law.[1] Before the public enterprises are formally privatized it is not possible to sell shares and therefore to start substantial privatization. Substantial privatization[2] is the divesture of public shares to private investors. Figure 4.1 illustrates the conceptualization of formal and substantial privatization.[3]

As discussed by Schuster et al. (2013) and Obinger et al. (2014), one of the central drawbacks of the existing empirical literature is the neglect of formal privatization (see also Chapter 3). Therefore, we have developed a new index that brings together the concept of formal and substantial privatization. This index relates the revenues of public enterprises to the Gross Domestic Product (GDP) on an annual basis. Hence, the Index of Public Entrepreneurship (IPE) measures the involvement of the state in the national economy and is calculated as follows:

$$IPE_{i,t} = \frac{\sum R^{DA}_{j,i,t} + \alpha \sum R^{PC}_{j,i,t} + \beta \sum R^{SC}_{j,i,t} * s^{SC}_{j,i,t}}{GDP_{i,t}}$$

DA: set of departmental agencies; PC: set of public corporations; SC: set of state companies; $R_{j,i,t}$: (total) revenues of a company j in a country i at time t; $S_{j,i,t}$: shares held by the state.

The index captures the type of organizational form (DA, PC, SC) and the percentage of shares owned by the government (S) on an annual basis and combines this information with the company's turnover for the given year (R). Formal and substantial privatization is weighted equally, whereas formal

---

[1] In the industrial sector, SOEs were often established as state companies, i.e. as companies subject to private law such as joint stock companies.
[2] Material and substantial privatization are used interchangeably.
[3] According to our conceptualization a state company becomes a private company when the state sells all public shares. Some scholars might argue that a company where the state is a minority shareholder (e.g. public shares <25 per cent or 50 per cent) can already be classified as a private company. However, this view neglects that the state might exercise control even as a minority shareholder via golden shares or ultimate ownership.

privatization is subdivided into two different types. When the state transforms a departmental agency into a public corporation (PC), then R_{PC} is weighted with α (here R_{DA} and R_{SC} are 0). α has to be smaller than 1 to indicate the retreat of the state and the enterprise's greater autonomy from political actors. The weighting for a transformation into a joint stock company is β. Since the possibilities for influencing the operational decisions of a joint stock company decrease for political actors in comparison to a public corporation (even though the state remains the unique shareholder), β has to be smaller than α. If the state additionally sells public shares (substantial privatization), the index value further decreases. When, for instance, 49 per cent of the public shares are divested, the weighting equals $\beta \times 0.51$ as the state still holds 51 per cent of the shares. Once a firm becomes completely privately owned (s=0), it drops out of the index. If more than one publicly owned firm operates in the sector then the index sums the weighted outputs over all firms. We weight formal and substantial privatization equally with formal privatization being subdivided into two different types. This means that α equals 0.75 and β 0.5.[4] The weighted outputs are finally set in reference to GDP.

To assess our Index of Public Entrepreneurship, we compiled a completely new database which contains data from all relevant public enterprises owned by the central government in twenty countries over the period between 1980 and 2007. To establish this database, information from national governments, regulatory agencies, national laws, and public enterprises was collected and analysed. Our analysis focuses on the national level only as compiling systematic data for public enterprises at the regional and local levels was impossible for twenty countries. Furthermore, the determinants of privatization at the subnational level are quite different from those at the national level. For example, the partisan complexion of government at the national level is irrelevant for the privatization of SOEs at the subnational level in federal systems.

The database includes information on 1,544 (formerly) public enterprises (such as turnover, number of employees, publicly held shares, etc.) from twenty OECD countries for the time period 1980–2007 (twenty-eight years). We gathered full time series for the two largest quintiles (in terms of turnover) since the upper two quintiles contribute at least 95 per cent of turnover and of all public enterprises. All monetary values are deflated to 2005 constant prices.[5] This information is used to calculate the IPE which is described in detail in Chapter 5.

---

[4] Since no theoretical justification for the selection of α and β exists, sensitivity analyses were applied in Chapter 5 using different weightings. The results in Chapter 5 do not change when using alternative weightings covering the broad range of possible weightings. Our findings are therefore not sensitive to different α's and β's.

[5] Data are available via Stefan Traub's personal website at http://www.hsu-hh.de/be/index_6xqlO0qRnxIqNp4Q.html.

Mapping the Size and Change of the Entrepreneurial State

Based on our dataset we are able to gauge the size of the public enterprise sector at the end of the so-called Golden Age of the interventionist state and the changes that occurred over the following almost three decades. Please note again that the size of the public sector refers to the central state level only so that particularly in federal countries the size of the SOE sector is larger when the subnational level is included.

Tables 4.1 and 4.2 show the development of the scope of privatization in the twenty OECD countries since 1980. Table 4.1 displays the Index of Public Entrepreneurship based on revenues (IPEr), whereas Table 4.2 reports the Index of Public Entrepreneurship based on employment figures (IPEe) which reflects the employment in SOEs in relation to the total national employment.

Both tables show a marked decline in the involvement of the state in entrepreneurial activities in nearly all countries over the last twenty-eight years. Governments throughout the OECD world launched comprehensive privatization programmes and divested public enterprises to the private sector.

The IPEr dropped on average from 6.25 per cent of GDP in 1980 to 3.05 per cent in 2007. Despite this overall downward trend, we can nonetheless observe remarkable cross-national differences. An extremely strong decline

Table 4.1. Index of public entrepreneurship: revenue (IPEr)

	Start value	End value	Change	Mean	SD
	1980	2007	1980–2007 (in %)	1980–2007	1980–2007
Australia	3.55	0.48	−86.48	2.42	1.04
Austria	7.75	3.03	−60.90	6.22	2.09
Belgium	4.70	1.92	−59.15	3.51	1.13
Canada	2.41	0.55	−77.18	1.45	0.85
Denmark	4.38	2.74	−37.44	3.41	0.79
Finland	8.63	6.93	−19.70	7.67	1.36
France	9.55	5.38	−43.66	8.32	1.99
Germany	3.21	1.41	−56.07	2.32	0.73
Greece	5.21	1.28	−75.43	2.90	1.30
Ireland	13.71	1.83	−86.65	6.30	3.74
Italy	6.45	2.17	−66.36	4.58	2.00
Japan	4.30	1.20	−72.09	2.75	0.90
Netherlands	7.83	2.20	−71.90	4.61	2.34
New Zealand	7.63	3.78	−50.46	3.95	2.37
Norway	6.82	13.36	95.89	11.66	1.62
Portugal	5.57	.90	−83.84	2.82	1.70
Spain	5.24	0.71	−86.45	2.61	1.70
Sweden	6.10	7.89	29.34	6.36	1.36
Switzerland	4.35	2.74	−37.01	4.23	1.01
UK	7.65	0.44	−94.25	2.45	2.53
Sample	6.25	3.05	−51.20	4.53	1.63

Source: REST Database

Table 4.2. Index of public entrepreneurship: employment (IPEe)

	Start value	End value	Change	Mean	SD
	1980	2007	1980–2007 (in %)	1980–2007	1980–2007
Australia	2.57	0.23	−91.05	1.36	0.96
Austria	2.45	0.56	−77.14	1.88	0.61
Belgium	3.61	0.74	−79.50	2.29	1.08
Canada	1.27	0.35	−72.44	0.65	0.30
Denmark	2.76	0.75	−72.83	1.97	0.85
Finland	4.85	1.64	−66.19	3.22	1.17
France	4.01	2.13	−46.88	3.51	0.92
Germany	4.01	0.58	−85.54	2.16	1.42
Greece	1.07	0.51	−52.34	0.84	0.23
Ireland	5.73	1.10	−80.80	2.86	1.50
Italy	3.09	0.59	−80.91	1.93	0.97
Japan	1.35	0.09	−93.33	0.67	0.34
Netherlands	2.51	0.21	−91.63	1.39	0.74
New Zealand	5.59	0.45	−91.95	0.86	0.41
Norway	4.19	2.53	−39.62	3.63	0.67
Portugal	1.44	0.33	−77.08	0.87	0.41
Spain	1.48	0.32	−78.38	0.96	0.45
Sweden	3.34	2.19	−34.43	2.76	0.62
Switzerland	2.86	1.27	−55.59	2.26	0.72
UK	4.25	0.37	−91.29	1.48	1.24
Sample	3.12	0.85	−72.94	1.89	0.81

Source: REST Database

of public entrepreneurship took place in the United Kingdom. While the turnover of state-owned enterprises was equivalent to 7.65 per cent of GDP in 1980, the public share was close to 0 in 2007. The same applies for Ireland where we observe the largest decline in absolute values from 13.71 in 1980 to 1.83 in 2007. Southern European countries such as Spain and Portugal also strongly relied on privatization. However, not all countries divested public enterprises on such a grand scale. In countries such as Switzerland and Denmark privatization was moderate, while in other countries the state plays an even greater role in business affairs than at the beginning of the period of observation. Norway is an extreme case in this respect, as the value of the index increased from 6.82 per cent in 1980 to 13.36 per cent in 2007. However, this development is mainly driven by a few big oil companies. For example, Norsk Hydro, a formerly majority-owned company involved in the oil business, significantly raised its turnover during the 1990s. Sweden and Finland also show an increase in public entrepreneurship in terms of the revenue-based index, albeit to a much lesser extent. Overall, the state has almost completely withdrawn from public enterprises in all English-speaking countries, whereas governments remained highly involved in entrepreneurial activities or even expanded their role in northern Europe.

A similar picture occurs for the IPEe based on employment figures. In contrast to the figures reported in Table 4.1, Japan, the Netherlands, and New Zealand cut back their involvement in public enterprises by about 90 per cent. This strong decline indicates that the state in these countries was a shareholder in highly overstaffed companies. The decline in public ownership is mainly mirrored in a declining number of employees in the respective firms and less with a decrease in revenues. The main difference to the revenue-based index reported in Table 4.1 is that the Nordic countries such as Norway and Sweden now also show a decline in public entrepreneurship—even though to a modest extent. This means that the increase in the Revenue Index in these countries was mainly driven by an increase in turnover rather than an increase in public shares. On average for all countries, the value of the Employment Index (IPEe) decreased from 3.12 in 1980 to 0.85 per cent in 2007. Most countries show a value close to 0 in 2007, indicating a strong retreat of public involvement into the economy.

The potential for privatization should vary strongly with the initial size of the public enterprise sector. In contrast to alternative indicators in the literature such as privatization revenues, our index makes it possible for the first time to measure a nation's stock of public enterprises and therefore to take the point of departure into account. Figure 4.2 maps the IPE (based on revenues) in 1980.

Figure 4.2 reveals several interesting facts. To begin with, there exist clear cross-national differences with respect to the size of the public enterprise

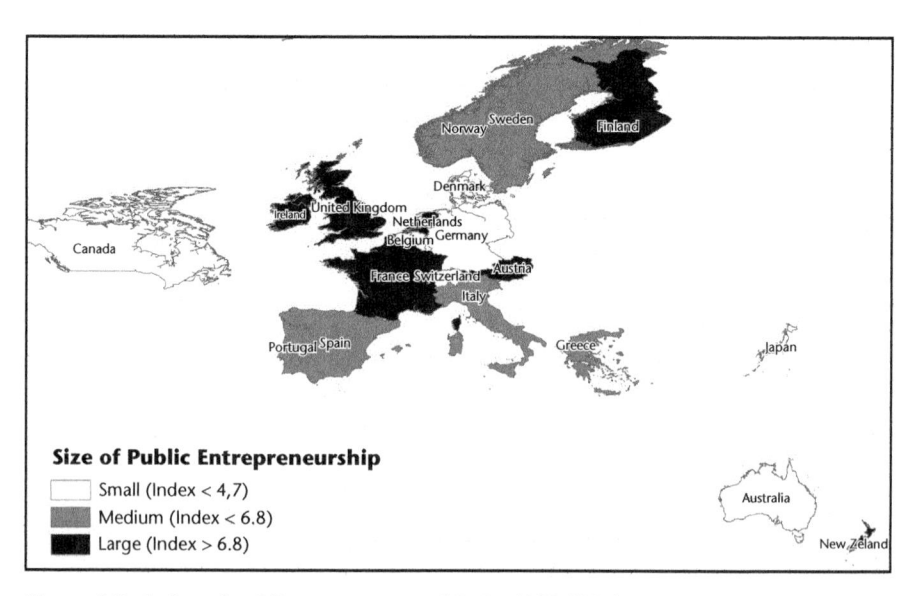

Figure 4.2. Index of public entrepreneurship in 1980 (IPEr)

Data and National Trajectories of Privatization

sector in 1980. For example, the IPEr ranges from 2.41 per cent in Canada to 13.71 per cent in Ireland and is therefore indicative of a huge variation within the English-speaking countries. While Canada and Australia did not have a large tradition of public entrepreneurship at the *national* level, the situation looks quite different in Ireland, New Zealand, and the United Kingdom where many big companies were publicly owned in the post-war period. Figure 4.2 shows that the initial size of the state-owned enterprise sector of these countries is comparable to France with its well-known state interventionist tradition. The Southern European and most of the Scandinavian countries range in between. Germany is also an interesting case as the initial size of the public enterprise sector at the central state level was rather small and similar to that in Canada and Australia. However, all three countries are federal states with large SOE sectors at the subnational level.

Figure 4.3 shows the *change* in public entrepreneurship between 1980 and 2007. The country clusters differ widely from those identified in Figure 4.2. Countries with high initial levels of public entrepreneurship did not necessarily embark on large-scale privatization. For example, despite substantial variation in the initial size of the public enterprise sector, all the English-speaking nations launched encompassing privatization programmes. Irrespective of varying policy legacies, all these countries considered privatization as the appropriate policy for reaching particular micro- and macro-economic objectives. On the other hand, countries with similar initial levels of public entrepreneurship in Southern Europe and Scandinavia followed wholly

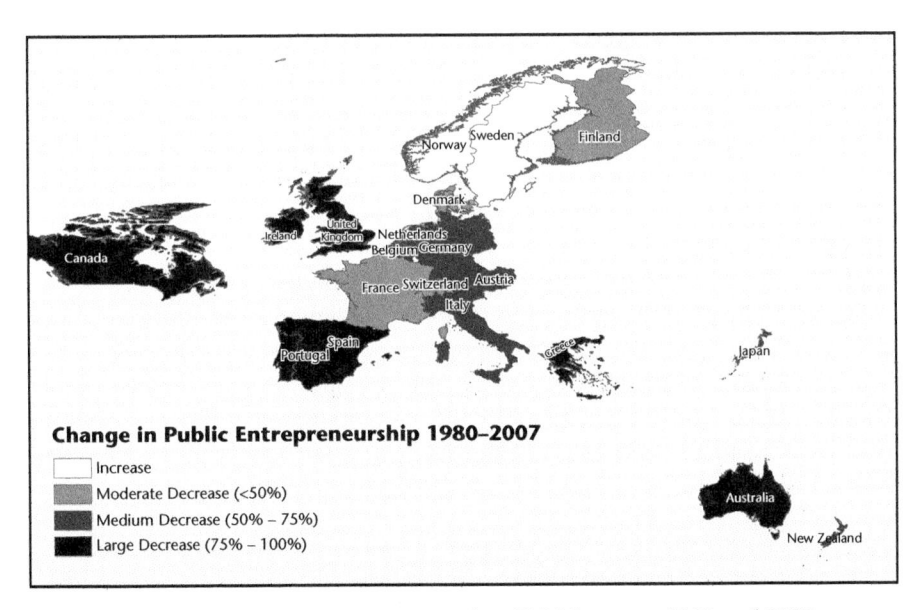

Change in Public Entrepreneurship 1980–2007
- Increase
- Moderate Decrease (<50%)
- Medium Decrease (50% – 75%)
- Large Decrease (75% – 100%)

Figure 4.3. Change in public entrepreneurship (IPEr) between 1980 and 2007

different policy routes over the last thirty years. While the Southern European countries strongly retreated from entrepreneurial activities, the influence of the state in the national economy remained rather substantial in much of Scandinavia. In contrast to the English-speaking countries and Southern Europe, the German-speaking countries as well as Belgium and the Netherlands only privatized to a moderate extent.

Figure 4.4 shows the country-specific development of both indices for different families of nations (Castles 1998).

The country-specific privatization trajectories indicate clear regional patterns irrespective of a considerable variation within some families of nations in terms of the initial size of the public enterprise sector. In the Scandinavian countries, the public involvement in the business sector remained relatively high throughout the whole period. This particularly holds true for the index based on revenues.[6] A rather homogenous trend can also be observed in Southern Europe as all countries started from a moderate level of public entrepreneurship in 1980 and ended up at low values in 2007. By contrast, the pattern of the English-speaking countries is different. As already indicated in Figure 4.3, these countries formed a very heterogeneous group in 1980, but converged towards very low index values until 2007. Likewise the countries in continental Europe were quite heterogeneous in the beginning with France and Austria at the top and Germany at the bottom of the group. With the notable exception of France, however, all countries converged to the German level over the period of observation.

Our data set also allows for a sector-specific breakdown of privatization activities. Since public utilities might show different patterns of privatization due to a typically two-staged privatization process, we have calculated separate indices for the main public utility sectors and for all remaining companies (= Industry). The index for the public utility sectors includes all companies in three main network-based utilities that are operated at the national level, namely the telecommunications, railways, and postal sectors.[7] Figure 4.5 illustrates the average development of the total and sector-specific Revenue Index between 1980 and 2007.

Again, we can observe an overall decline of the public enterprise sector over time. Interestingly, however, this trend is particularly pronounced in the public utility sectors. For the remaining companies, public ownership is also on the retreat, but the decline is not as strong as in the public utility sectors. On average, public involvement in the network-based industries declined from slightly above 3 per cent of the GDP in 1980 to 1 per cent in 2007. The IPEr for the remaining sectors only declined from 3 to 2 per cent.

---

[6] As mentioned, the Norwegian figures are highly driven by the high turnover of oil companies.
[7] Other public utility sectors such as electricity and water supply are provided at the regional or local level in many countries.

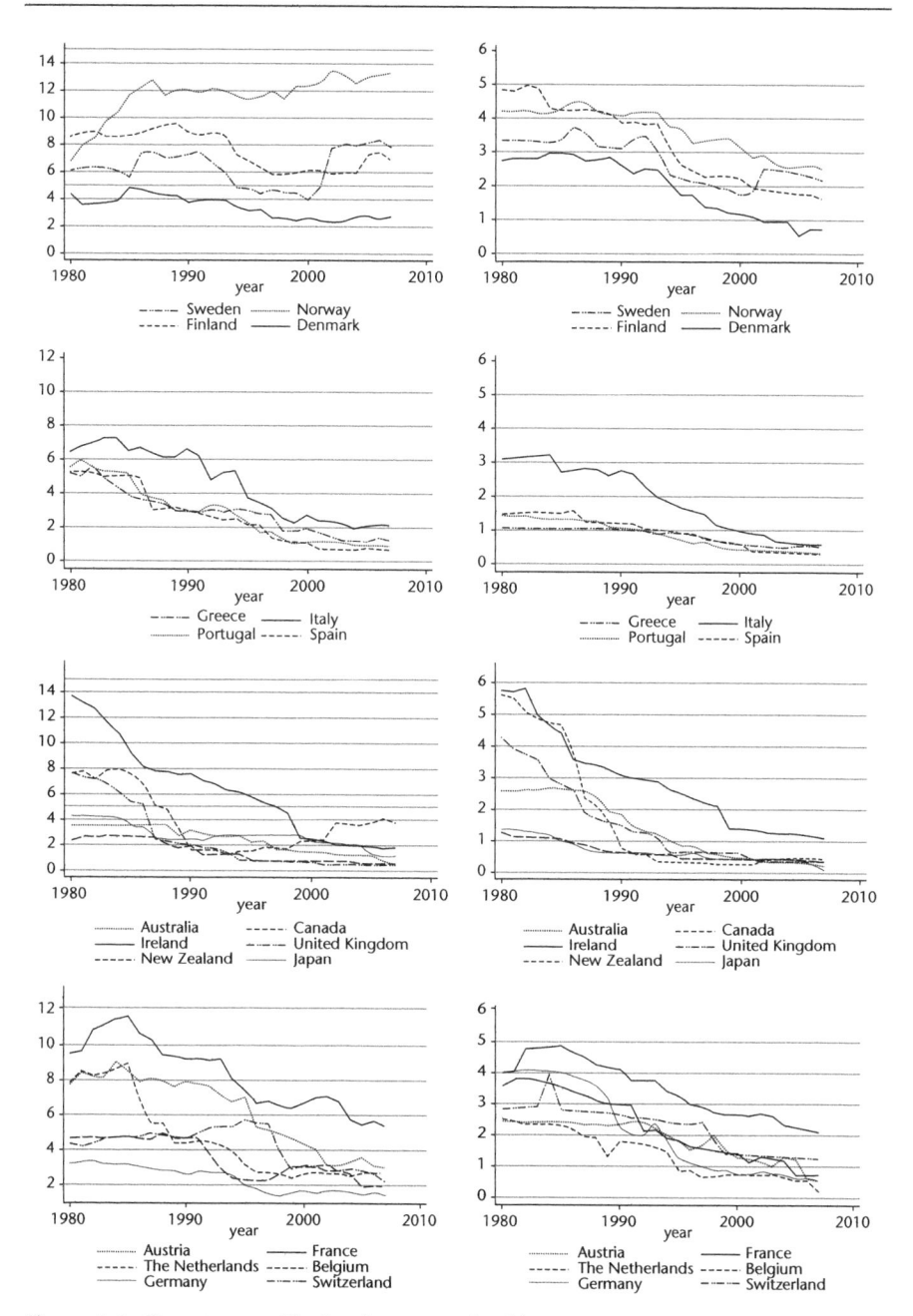

Data and National Trajectories of Privatization

Figure 4.4. Country-specific development of public entrepreneurship (IPE)
Notes: IPEr (Revenue Index, left-hand side) and IPEe (Employment Index, right-hand side)

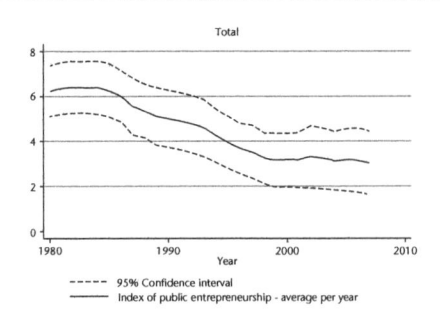

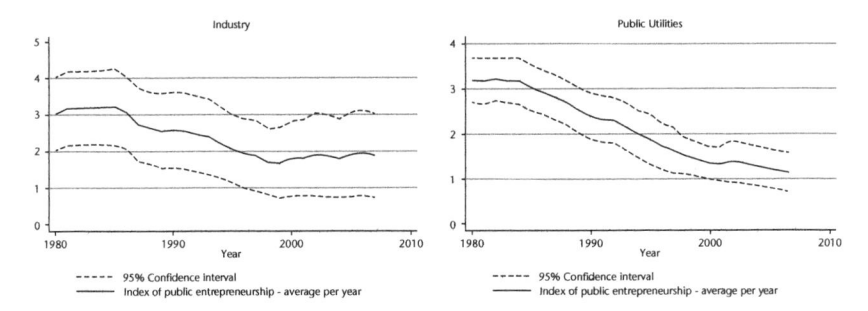

Political Economy of Privatization in Rich Democracies

Figure 4.5. Average sector development of IPEr

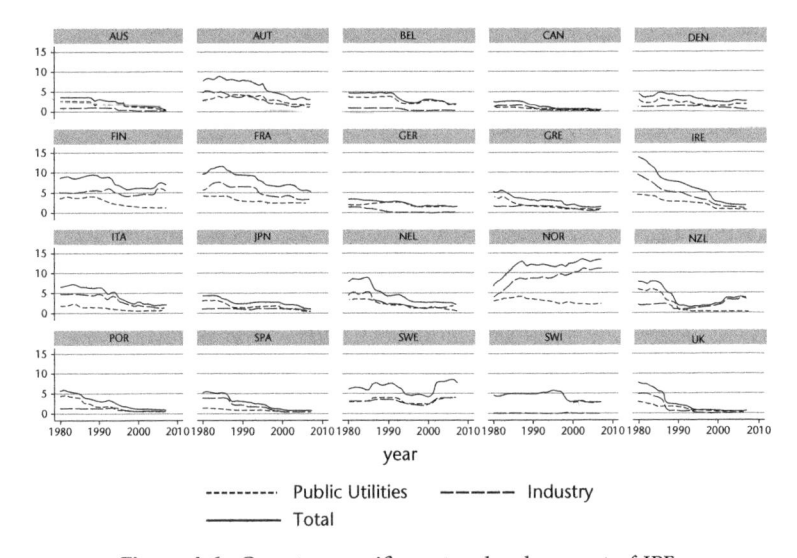

Figure 4.6. Country-specific sector development of IPEr

Since Figure 4.5 almost certainly masks a considerable cross-national variation, Figure 4.6 illustrates the development of these indices in all twenty countries.

In fact, there exist large cross-sector differences between countries. In Switzerland, for example, the government has been and still is mainly involved in

Data and National Trajectories of Privatization

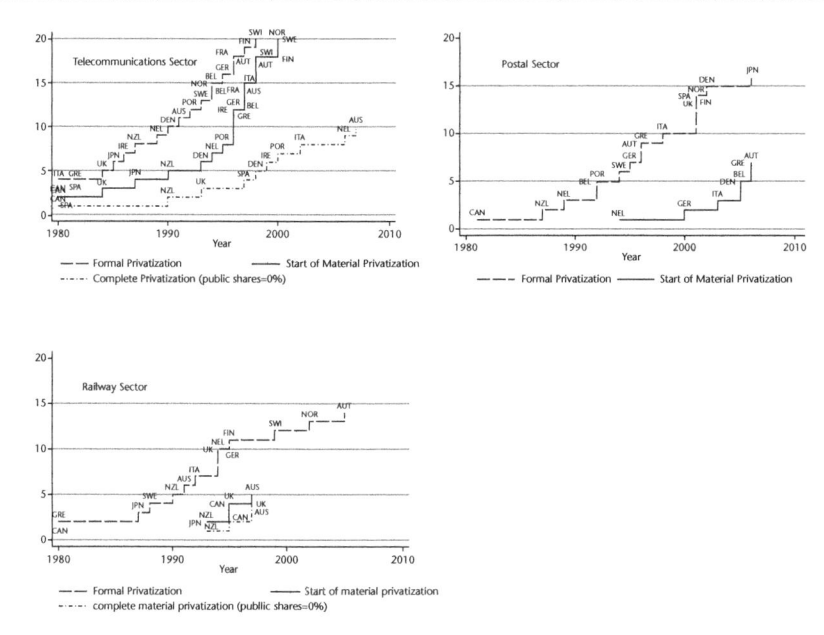

Figure 4.7. Sector-specific privatization trajectories

the public utility sectors, notably railways. By contrast, there are only a few industrial companies in public hands. In Norway, the total index is very largely driven by the oil industry, whereas the decline of public utilities is much in line with the development in other countries. Other countries such as the United Kingdom and Ireland are equally involved in the industrial and public utility sectors or show similar developments in both sectors. Moreover, the timing of privatization differs across countries. In Germany and Austria public utility providers were privatized later than industrial companies, while Denmark has privatized the public utility sectors earlier than the industrial sector.

Figure 4.7 illustrates the privatization trajectories in three public utility sectors (postal, telecommunications, and railway services) in greater detail operating at the national level.[8] More specifically, Figure 4.7 distinguishes between formal and substantial privatization as well as by sector. The horizontal axis indicates the time dimension whereas the vertical axis displays the cumulative number of countries which have either completed the formal privatization process or where the respective provider has been a private law company from the very outset (dashed line). In addition, the cumulative number of countries is presented which have begun the substantial

---

[8] When using the term public utilities, we only refer to these three sectors.

67

privatization process (solid line) or have already finished substantial privatization by selling all public shares (dotted line).

Figure 4.7 shows impressively that besides a general retreat from public service provision in all three sectors, there are remarkable cross-country and cross-sector differences. The privatization process has moved most strongly to completion in the telecommunications sector.[9] All twenty countries have formally privatized their telecommunications provider and have commenced the material privatization process. In ten countries, the telecommunications provider is today completely operated by private companies. In the railways sector, by contrast, formal privatization has not been implemented in all countries and only New Zealand, the United Kingdom, and Japan have divested public shares. Privatization activities are still less pronounced in the postal sector since the formal privatization process started later than in the other two sectors and none of the twenty OECD countries has completely divested its postal provider. To date, only members of the EU have commenced the divestment of public shares in the postal sector. Hence this process seems to be driven by the European integration. In contrast, in the telecommunications sector, formal and material privatization is a common trend across the entire OECD world. The divesture of the telecommunications providers is highly profitable and offers a possibility for policy makers to easily raise large amounts of revenue. Figure 4.7 also shows that the English-speaking countries were among the early birds with respect to privatization, at least regarding the telecommunications and railway sectors. By contrast, the Scandinavian and German-speaking countries formally and materially privatized their public utility providers relatively late.

Summary

Based on a new data base and a conceptualization of privatization that takes formal and material privatization into account, this chapter has described the extent and development of public entrepreneurship in twenty countries over the last thirty years. We have identified the following general patterns and pathways.

First, the initial size of public entrepreneurship in 1980 differed widely across countries. While in some countries such as the United Kingdom and France the state was highly involved in the national economy, in other countries such as Canada and Germany state-owned enterprises were far less present at the national level.

---

[9] For Canada, the information refers to Bell Canada as the largest national telecommunications provider.

Second, almost all countries have divested public enterprises since 1980. However, the overall picture is more heterogeneous than expected. For example, the English-speaking countries almost completely retreated from entrepreneurial activities irrespective of the very distinct initial size of their public enterprise sectors. In contrast, the intrusion of government into the national economy remained high in the Scandinavian countries over the last thirty years.

Third, and quite surprising, a general retreat of the state across all countries is primarily observable in the public utility sectors. Despite this common withdrawal from network-based utilities, the development of public entrepreneurship is quite different across sectors. While all states have privatized their national telecommunications providers, the privatization process in the postal and railways sectors has proceeded more slowly as in most countries these companies are still under public control.

Fourth, countries maintain particular strategic sectors. Switzerland, for example, is mainly involved in the public utility sectors but only has a few industrial companies. In contrast, Norway is highly involved in the oil industry, whereas the public utility sectors play a minor role.

Finally, countries do not only differ with regard to the extent of privatization and sector-specific priorities, but also in terms of the timing of privatization. English-speaking countries were typically among the early birds, while the privatization of state-owned enterprises generally started later in continental and northern Europe.

In sum, there is a considerable variation across countries and sectors. Explaining these different patterns and pathways of privatization is the key purpose of Chapter 5.

5

The Determinants of Privatization

Empirical Findings

Using multivariate regression analysis and spatial econometrics, this chapter examines the determinants of privatization in twenty advanced democracies between 1980 and 2007. Particular emphasis is devoted to the impact of political parties and the role played by political and legal institutions. Moreover, we examine whether and to which extent privatization was shaped by policy diffusion. We proceed in five steps. In a first section, we investigate whether privatization activities in advanced democracies led to policy convergence over time. Next, we study how different constitutional settings have influenced the scope and timing of privatization. The following section investigates the impact of political parties on privatizing state-owned enterprises, whereas the next section examines whether privatization can be attributed to policy diffusion. The final section provides a summary of the major empirical findings.

Convergence Analysis

As we have seen in Chapter 3, privatization activities are often attributed to economic globalization, Europeanization, the collapse of the Soviet bloc, the spread of neo-liberal ideas, or fiscal problem pressure. As many or even all countries were affected by these occurrences and problems, all these factors are imputed causes of convergence.[1] By contrast, path dependency, domestic

---

[1] Holzinger and Knill (2005) distinguish between five potential triggers of convergence, namely independent problem solving (e.g. independent response of governments to fiscal pressure and/or economic inefficiencies of SOEs), transnational communication (e.g. the travelling of neo-liberal ideas, the exchange of information, policy learning), international harmonization (Europeanization), competition (e.g. regulatory competition caused by globalization), and imposition.

politics, and country-specific problem pressures are seen as crucial in explaining the persistence of cross-national differences in economic policies or even as forces making for further divergence in the size of the public enterprise sector. Generally speaking, convergence denotes increasing similarity of policies over time. However, convergence is a multifaceted concept with four types of convergence distinguished in the literature (see Knill 2005: 768–9; Heichel et al. 2005: 831–4). In this section, we focus on sigma and beta-convergence as the most important types of convergence in empirical research.

Sigma Convergence

The most common and simplest approach to analyse convergence is to compare the variation of policies at two points in time. A decline in statistical measures of dispersion, such as the standard deviation or the coefficient of variation, is denoted as sigma-convergence. Table 5.1 summarizes descriptive statistics for our two indices of public entrepreneurship at four points in time.

Interestingly, there is no clear evidence of sigma convergence. Comparing the coefficient of variation over time suggests that countries have even become more heterogeneous over the last thirty years. With regard to the Revenue Index, the coefficient of variation increased from 0.42 in 1980 to 1.05 in 2007. A similar divergence can be observed if we look at the standard deviation of the Revenue Index. These findings are mainly driven by a sharp decline of the mean and the deviating policy trend in the Scandinavian countries, notably Norway. Only the standard deviation of the Employment Index declined over time. Overall, however, this evidence is not supportive of a convergence towards a common equilibrium, even though the bulk of countries have significantly retreated from entrepreneurial activities.

Table 5.1. Index of public entrepreneurship: descriptive statistics

Index of public entrepreneurship	1980	1990	2000	2007
IPEr (revenue)				
Mean	6.25	5.01	3.18	3.05
Minimum	2.41	1.63	0.72	0.44
Maximum	13.71	12.07	12.38	13.36
Standard deviation	2.60	2.96	2.69	3.20
Coefficient of variation	0.42	0.59	0.85	1.05
IPEe (employment)				
Mean	3.12	2.22	1.14	0.85
Minimum	1.07	0.63	0.28	0.10
Maximum	5.73	4.16	3.16	2.53
Standard deviation	1.41	1.13	0.80	0.73
Coefficient of variation	0.45	0.51	0.70	0.86

A further test on sigma convergence is to run a regression of the standard deviation and the coefficient of variation on time. The results reported in Table 5.2 support the findings of Table 5.1 as the coefficients of the time variable are positive and statistically significant in three out of four models. This means that the standard deviation and the coefficient of variation significantly increased over time. Apart from column 2 (standard deviation of IPEe) we can observe a divergence trend. These results remain stable even when excluding Norway from the sample.

Looking at the public utility sector and the industrial sector separately (Table 5.3) reveals an interesting picture. While the findings for the industrial sector by and large are indicative of divergence, the impact of the time variable on the standard deviation of the Revenue and Employment Index is Negative in the public utility sectors. In other words, there is evidence of convergence in these network-based sectors. Once more, the Nordic countries play a crucial role in this finding. The expansion of the public oil industry in Norway, for example, led to an increase of the Revenue Index that contributed to growing cross-national heterogeneity in the industrial sector. By contrast, the development in the public utility sectors in the Nordic countries was much in line with that in other countries.

Beta Convergence

While sigma convergence focuses on cross-sectional dispersion, beta convergence denotes an inverse relationship between the initial value of a particular policy indicator and its subsequent change. This concept of convergence is thus equivalent to a catch-up or catch-down process towards a common

Table 5.2. Regression on time

	Standard deviation		Coefficient of variation	
	IPEr	IPEe	IPEr	IPEe
Constant	−27.66***	56.70***	−50.75***	−30.76***
	(7.67)	(2.20)	(1.62)	(1.46)
Year	0.015***	−0.028***	0.025***	0.016***
	(0.004)	(0.001)	(0.001)	(0.001)
R^2	0.35	0.95	0.97	0.94
F	15.79***	641.33***	1011.85***	462.07
N	560	560	560	560

Notes: *** $p<0.01$, ** $p<0.05$, * $p<0.1$; standard errors in parentheses

Table 5.3. Regression on time separated by sector

Industry	Standard deviation		Coefficient of variation	
	IPEr	IPEe	IPEr	IPEe
Constant	−16.38***	30.48***	−58.67***	−29.38***
	(1.38)	(0.283)	(0.533)	(0.601)
Year	0.009***	−0.015***	0.030***	0.015***
	(0.0007)	(0.0001)	(0.0002)	(0.0003)
R^2	0.25	0.95	0.96	0.82
F	184.66***	11160.22***	12568.8***	2517.05***
N	560	560	560	560

Notes: *** p<0.01, ** p<0.05, * p<0.1; standard errors in parentheses

Public Utilities	Standard Deviation		Coefficient of Variation	
	IPEr	IPEe	IPEr	IPEe
Constant	−17.86***	55.77***	−38.18***	−20.27***
	(0.927)	(2.20)	(1.62)	(1.46)
Year	−0.008***	−0.028***	0.019***	0.010***
	(0.0004)	(0.001)	(0.0002)	(0.001)
R^2	0.35	0.57	0.94	0.36
F	327.18***	746.09***	8536.28***	213.37***
N	560	560	560	560

Notes: *** p<0.01, ** p<0.05, * p<0.1; standard errors in parentheses

equilibrium in the long run. A simple test for beta convergence is to regress the start value of a particular policy indicator on its subsequent change in a cross-section model. If the estimated coefficient for the initial value has a negative sign and is statistically significant, there is evidence of absolute beta-convergence. Conditional beta-convergence occurs when the coefficient of the initial value only takes a negative sign if additional variables are controlled for.

We use Error Correction Models (ECMs) as the most suitable modelling strategy for testing this type of convergence. Dynamic models such as ECMs have the advantage compared to cross-section analyses that they 'allow us to estimate and test for both short- and long-run effects' in a single equation (De Boef and Keele 2008: 191).[2] Since ECMs assume the existence of a long-term equilibrium which defines the ultimate state to which the units converge over

---

[2] ECMs were originally developed for non-stationary data and are usually associated with co-integrated time series. De Boef and Keele (2008), however, show analytically and with simulated data that ECMs are also appropriate for stationary data since ECMs are equivalent to autoregressive distributed lag models which has a stationarity condition.

time, it is particularly suitable to test the theoretical predictions of convergence theory.[3]

The dependent variable is the annual percentage change in the level of public entrepreneurship. The independent variables enter ECMs with their lagged levels and their first differences. The empirical analysis proceeds as follows. In a first step, we test for absolute or unconditional convergence and estimate models that only include the lagged level of our index (Models I and IV). In a second step, we analyse conditional convergence with (Models III and VI) and without (Models II and V) country dummies. Hence we present three estimations for each index (cf. Table 5.4). The regressions without country dummies address the question whether the countries in our sample converge to the same equilibrium after controlling for important economic and political variables. The regressions with country dummies take unobserved heterogeneity into account by allowing for different intercepts. Including country dummies enables us to test whether countries converge to a country-specific equilibrium.

We control for several political and economic variables that might influence the convergence process and have been identified in the empirical literature as determinants of privatization and were broadly discussed in Chapter 3. For the measurement of these variables and data sources see Table A.2 in the appendix.

Table 5.4 summarizes the empirical results for the overall index for public entrepreneurship. Note that the change in the index of public entrepreneurship, i.e. our dependent variable, is negative when the state retreats from entrepreneurial activities.

In contrast to the findings for the sigma convergence reported in Tables 5.1 and 5.2, the findings of the multivariate analyses strongly support the existence of beta convergence. Countries not only converge to a country-specific but also to a cross-country equilibrium. While absolute beta convergence is restricted to the Employment Index (Model IV), the results of Models II, III, V, and VI unequivocally point to the presence of conditional convergence: the higher the previous level of public entrepreneurship, the stronger was, ceteris paribus, its decline. Apart from this catch-down process, the long-term effects of the control variables are interesting in several respects. As expected, high levels of public debt accelerate privatizations, while strong left governments consistently impede a retreat of the state from entrepreneurial activities. The impact of trade openness is negative and statistically significant in the models including country dummies. This evidence supports the efficiency thesis more than the compensation logic. We find inconsistent results for the long-term

---

[3] The general equation is: $\Delta Y_t = a_0 - a_1(Y_{t-1} - \beta_1 X_t - 1) + \beta_0 \Delta X_t + \epsilon_t$; β_0 captures any immediate (short-term) effect that X has on Y. β_1 reflects the long-term impact of X on Y. The rate of realization of the long-term effect across future time periods is determined by the error correction rate a_1.

Table 5.4. Beta convergence: error correction models

Variable	IPEr (revenue)			IPEe (employment)		
	I	II	III	IV	V	VI
IPE public entrepreneurship$_{t-1}$	−0.010	−0.021**	−0.134***	−0.032***	−0.035***	−0.123***
	(0.011)	(0.011)	(0.015)	(0.010)	(0.010)	(0.011)
Δ GDP per capita (log.)	–	−1.58*	−1.43	–	−0.705***	−0.594**
		(0.893)	(0.952)		(0.223)	(0.249)
GDP per capita (log.)	–	0.268***	−0.096	–	−0.010	−0.260***
		(0.050)	(0.255)		(0.035)	(0.043)
Δ Public debt	–	−0.008**	−0.007**	–	0.0002	−0.001
		(0.015)	(0.004)		(0.001)	(0.001)
Public debt	–	−0.002***	−0.005***	–	−0.0005***	−0.002***
		(0.001)	(0.0008)		(0.0001)	(0.0001)
Δ Trade openness	–	−0.014	−0.013	–	−0.009***	−0.010***
		(0.011)	(0.011)		(0.002)	(0.002)
Trade openness	–	−0.001	−0.007*	–	0.0002	−0.003***
		(0.001)	(0.004)		(0.0002)	(0.0004)
Δ Left-leaning cabinet	–	0.0007	0.0003	–	−0.00003	−0.0003
		(0.0008)	(0.0007)		(0.0002)	(0.0002)
Left-leaning cabinet	–	0.001***	0.001**	–	0.0004***	0.0003**
		(0.0005)	(0.006)		(0.0001)	(0.0001)
Δ Union density	–	0.011	−0.008	–	0.011***	0.006
		(0.015)	(0.015)		(0.004)	(0.004)
Union density	–	0.003***	0.003	–	0.0002	−0.006***
		(0.0008)	(0.006)		(0.0002)	(0.0007)
Δ Political institutions	–	0.781*	0.435	–	0.358**	0.225
		(0.463)	(0.514)		(0.144)	(0.181)
Political institutions	–	0.429	0.410	–	−0.009	−0.137
		(0.285)	(0.502)		(0.100)	(0.172)
Country dummies	No	No	Yes	No	No	Yes
R^2	0.002	0.08	0.20	0.04	0.09	0.17
WaldChi	0.82	456.48	2710.87***	10.58***	956.24***	4991.3***
N	540	484	484	540	484	484

Notes: *** z, $p<0.01$, ** z, $p<0.05$, * z, $p<0.1$; the fixed effects are suppressed to conserve space; standard errors in parentheses

impact of economic wealth and union density. No long-term effect whatsoever can be detected for institutional constraints.

In terms of the short-term effects of the controls, we find that high budget deficits lower the IPEr (i.e. speed up privatization), while an increase in trade openness has a similar effect for the IPEe. Economic growth turns out as a significant accelerating factor of privatization in three models. The impact of parties and unions is mostly insignificant in the short run, while the impact of political institutions is consistently positive and significant in two equations. This is much in line with theory as partisan effects typically take effect over the long term, whereas institutional constraints impede rapid and comprehensive policy change in the short run.

Tables 5.5 and 5.6 show the results for the ECMs differentiated between public utilities and industry. The estimated coefficients for the control

Table 5.5. Error correction models for the IPEr (revenue), separated by sector

Variable	IPEr			IPEr		
	industry			public utilities		
Lag of index	−0.008 0.010	−0.018*** 0.006	−0.109*** 0.015	−0.032*** 0.013	−0.039* 0.022	−0.215*** 0.033
Control variables	No	Yes	Yes	No	Yes	Yes
Country dummies	No	No	Yes	No	No	Yes
R^2	0.002	0.08	0.218	0.02	0.05	0.15
Wald Chi	0.66	1809.45***	11642.95***	6.51***	88.08	586.53***
N	540	484	484	540	484	484

Notes: *** z, p<0.01, ** z, p<0.05, * z, p<0.1; the fixed effects are suppressed to conserve space; standard errors in parentheses

Table 5.6. Error correction models for the IPEe (employment), separated by sector

Variable	IPEe			IPEe		
	industry			public utilities		
Lag of index	−0.033*** 0.008	−0.042*** 0.005	−0.106*** 0.010	−0.032*** 0.013	−0.039* 0.022	−0.215*** 0.033
Control variables	No	Yes	Yes	No	Yes	Yes
Country dummies	No	No	Yes	No	No	Yes
R^2	0.07	0.11	0.19	0.02	0.05	0.15
Wald Chi	17.46***	1860.12***	67585.53***	6.51**	88.08***	586.53***
N	540	484	484	540	484	484

Notes: *** z, p<0.01, ** z, p<0.05, * z, p<0.1; the fixed effects are suppressed to conserve space; standard errors in parentheses

variables do not differ substantially from the results presented in Table 5.4 and are therefore suppressed to conserve space.

Comparing the results of both tables, it becomes clear that the lack of absolute beta convergence in the case of the IPEr (cf. Table 5.4, Model I) is apparently caused by the development in the industrial sector and not by the public utility sectors. Again, this result is mainly driven particularly by the Nordic countries such as Norway where the public oil industry has grown largely over the last decades.

Constitutional Framework and Privatization of Public Utilities

We have seen in the previous section that political institutions, understood as institutional veto points, are obstacles to policy change in the short run. However, the general institutional indices used in the literature are rather crude proxies to map the institutionally preconfigured room to manoeuvre of political actors. What is needed is a policy-specific measure that captures institutional barriers against privatization. Of particular importance in this respect are constitutional provisions related to public utilities. As demonstrated in Chapter 2, the public provision of network-based infrastructures has been a core attribute of modern statehood in almost all advanced democracies after the Second World War. The political and economic importance of these sectors was often mirrored by constitutional provisions that granted these sectors a special legal status in many OECD countries. Because of this special constitutional status, the privatization of public utilities required comprehensive legal changes which often included constitutional amendments. Hence our basic argument is that different constitutional settings influence both the timing and the extent of privatizations as they constitute different legal barriers in the privatization process. Countries with a constitutional framework including many barriers for privatization should need more time to implement privatization programmes. This holds true for formal and material privatizations alike so that both types of privatization have to be taken into account.

In fact, the legal status of public utilities differed widely among rich democracies (Ambrosius 2000: 18; Püttner 1985; Graham and Prosser 2003). For example, the term *service public* in the French Constitution is of essential importance and reflects a particular state and administration doctrine (Krajewski et al. 2009; Braconnier 2003; Dreyfus 2009). The preamble to the French Constitution of 1946 stipulates 'that all property and all enterprises that have or that may acquire the character of a public service or de facto monopoly shall become the property of society' (Ambrosius 2000: 19). However, public utilities have not everywhere gained a similar relevance in the legal order. While the classic network-based infrastructures in the German-speaking countries were of similar size and enjoyed a similar monopoly position, there was no cohesive legal conception of public utilities comparable to the French notion of public services. Nevertheless, sectors such as postal services, railways, and telecommunications enjoyed a special constitutional status in countries such as Germany and Switzerland (Ambrosius 2000; Hellermann 2001). In contrast to France and Germany, there is no public law in the United Kingdom defining particular state functions and their implementation. Even though public utilities were supplied by state-owned enterprises during the post-war period, this did not happen under the umbrella of a constitutionally protected jurisdiction of government (Graham and Prosser 2003; Bell 2007; Glenn 2007).

By integrating insights from law and public administration, we developed together with experts in constitutional law a list of constitutional provisions that from a theoretical point of view might constrain the possibilities for privatization. For example, the staff of state-owned enterprises was often made up of public employees and civil servants. If a constitution contains comprehensive provisions concerning the public service or if it actually guarantees tenure or a right to resist a transfer of personnel, policy makers have to find solutions in line with the constitution when they aim at privatizing public enterprises. Privatizations would also be difficult to achieve if a constitution stipulates that service provision is a matter of government (see Schmitt and Obinger 2011 for a more detailed discussion of other relevant constitutional provisions). In a next step, we generated a questionnaire which was sent to legal scientists and country experts in the respective constitutional law. These country experts were asked to gauge the presence and importance of these constitutional barriers in their national settings. The experts were also requested to indicate changes over time in the period from 1980 until 2010. Table 5.7 summarizes the eight components of our index and their measurement.

Based on the completed questionnaires, we compiled a new data set from which an index of constitutional barriers against privatization was developed. Each of the eight indicators was normalized, thus ranging from 0 to 1. The index of constitutional barriers is a simple additive index from 0 to 8. If the constitutional barriers of a country changed over time, we calculated the index for each period in relation to the total period of observation and added all sub-indices. Table 5.8 shows the values for every sub-indicator for each country and the resulting index of constitutional barriers.

Figure 5.1 and Figure 5.2 reveal a considerable cross-national variation of institutional obstacles against privatization. Overall, governments in Southern Europe, France, and German-speaking countries are confronted with many constitutional barriers. But while countries in Southern Europe show

Determinants of Privatization: Empirical Findings

Table 5.7. Constitutional barriers to privatization: components and measurement

Category		Coding
1. Role of the constitution		(0) Formal precedent of constitution
		(1) No formal precedent of constitution
		(0) Substantial influence of the constitution
		(1) No substantial influence of the constitution
		(0) No constitutional court
		(0.5) Strong position courts
		(1) Constitutional court
2. State principles	Democracy	(0) No (1) Yes
	Rule of law	(0) No (1) Yes
	Federalism	(0) No (1) Yes
	Welfare state	(0) No (1) Yes
	Republic	(0) No (1) Yes
	Public services	(0) No (1) Yes
3. State duties		(0) No (1) Yes
4. General regulations on privatization		(0) No (1) Yes
5. General regulations on public utilities		(0) No (1) Yes
6. Regulations on postal, telecommunications, and railway services		(0) No constitutional requirements
		(0.5) Sector is assigned to the legislative jurisdiction of the government
		(1) Guarantee of adequate public service provision
7. Social rights	Right to work	(0) No (1) Yes
	Right to education	(0) No (1) Yes
	Right to housing	(0) No (1) Yes
	Right to health	(0) No (1) Yes
	Right to social security	(0) No (1) Yes
	Right to culture	(0) No (1) Yes
	Right to safe environment	(0) No (1) Yes
8. Civil service		(0) No regulations
		(0.5) Constitutional guarantees
		(1) Comprehensive constitutional guarantees

high values with respect to the civil service, social rights, state duties, and state principles, German-speaking countries score particularly highly in terms of sector-specific regulations. By contrast, constitutional barriers are relatively low in the English-speaking and Nordic countries.

We hypothesize that the differences in the scope of privatization across OECD countries are shaped by these different constitutional settings. The more barriers are anchored in a constitution the lower should be the intensity of privatization. To test our argument that constitutional barriers hamper the privatization of public utilities, we selected three classic public utility sectors which, in addition, are typically operated at the national level, i.e. the postal

Table 5.8. Constitutional barriers to privatization in twenty OECD countries, 1980–2007

Country	Role of constitution	State principles	State duties	General regulations	Regulation on public utilities	Sector regulations	Social rights	Civil service	Index of constitutional barriers
Australia	1	0.33	0	0	0.17	0.5	0	0	2
Austria	1	0.58	0	0	1	0.5	0.14	0.5	3.73
Belgium	0.67	0.33	1	0	1	0.5	0.14	0	3.64
Canada	0.67	0.17	0	0	0.33	0.5	0	0	1.67
Denmark	0	0.25	0	0	0	0	0.43	0.5	1.18
Finland	0.33	0.42	0	0	0	0	0.07	0.5	1.32
France	0.67	0.83	0	1	0	0	0.71	0.5	3.71
Germany	1	1	1	0	1	1	0.14	1	7.04
Greece	0.67	0.33	1	0	0	0	0.71	0	3.71
Ireland	1	0.67	0	0	0	0	0.57	0	2.24
Italy	1	1	1	1	0	0	0.57	0.5	5.07
Japan	0.67	0.5	1	0	0	0	0.5	0	2.67
Netherlands	0.67	0.17	0	0	0	0	0.29	0.25	1.37
New Zealand	0.33	0.5	0	0	0	0	0.43	0	1.26
Norway	0.5	0.33	0	0	0	0	0		5.17
Portugal	0.33	0.83	1	1	0	0	1	1	5.17
Spain	1	0.83	1	0	0.83	0.5	1	1	6.17
Sweden	0.5	0.5	0	0	0	0	0	0	1.71
Switzerland	0.67	0.5	1	1	1	1	0.71	0	5.17
United Kingdom	0	0.3	0	0	0	0	0	0	0.33

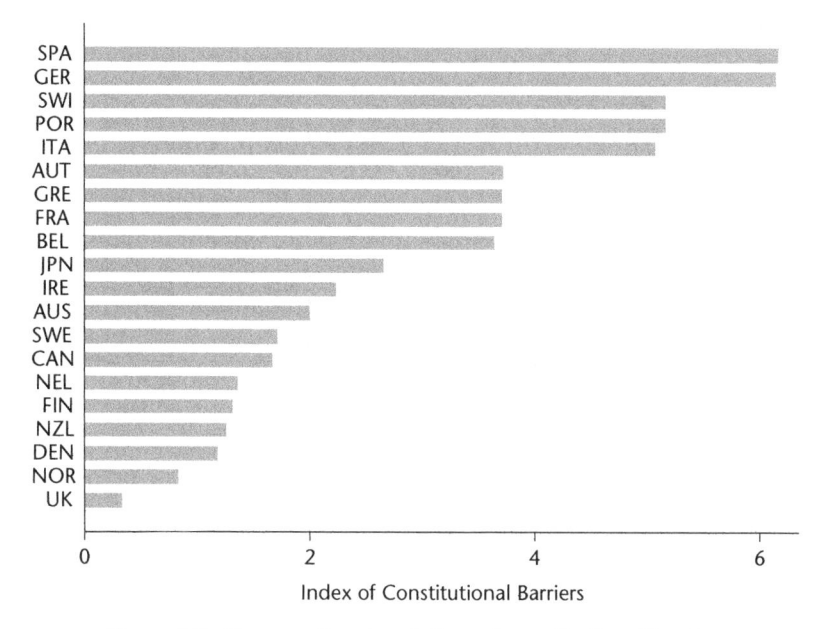

Determinants of Privatization: Empirical Findings

Figure 5.1. Cross-national variation of constitutional barriers

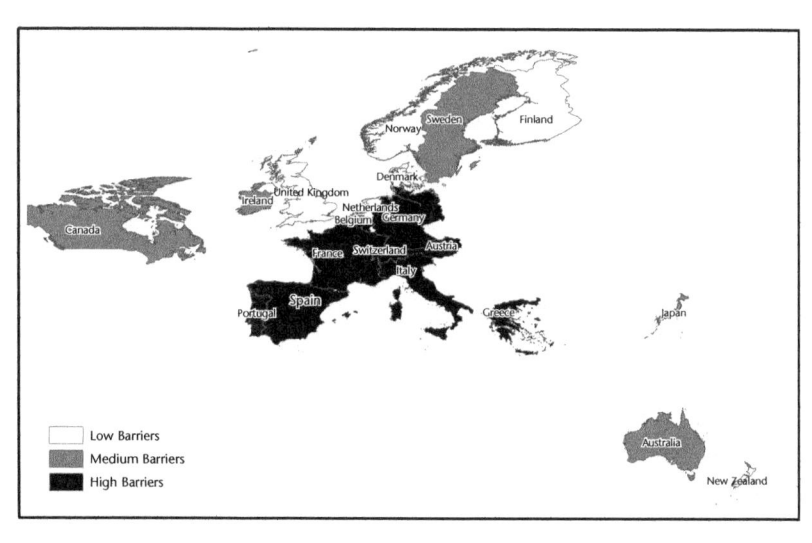

Figure 5.2. A map of constitutional barriers

sector, telecommunications, and railways service.[4] To gauge the impact of constitutional provisions on privatization we rely on a novel dependent variable. In an effort to take into account the entire privatization process,

---

[4] Due to European legislation, the railway network was separated from passenger transportation and freight traffic. We focus on passenger transportation in this book.

Political Economy of Privatization in Rich Democracies

we sum up the values of our index of public entrepreneurship[5] from 1980 until 2007.

$$Public\ Involvement = \sum_{1980}^{2007} X^{DA} + \alpha * X^{PC} + \beta * X^{SC} * s^{SC}$$

X^{DA}: 1 = departmental agency; 0 = other organizational form; X^{PC}: 1 = public corporation; 0 = other organizational form; X^{SC}: 1 = state company; 0 = other organizational form; α: weighting for formal privatization, (DA→PC); β: weighting for formal privatization, (PC→SC); s^{SC}: shares held by the state.

The variable 'Public Involvement' has the advantage that it captures the timing and the extent of privatizations simultaneously. Since we do not argue that constitutional barriers impede privatizations but rather make privatizations more difficult, the pure extent of privatization would be misleading. We rather hypothesize that constitutional barriers influence the speed of privatization, i.e. whether a country is able to implement privatizations quickly or whether the privatization process is protracted. To make this clear, consider a country which privatizes the telecommunications provider early on. In this case, the public involvement in this sector and therefore the index would be relatively low compared to a country which privatizes its telecommunications provider at the end of the period under investigation.

The empirical findings are reported in Table 5.9. Models I to III use the scope of the public involvement in each sector as the dependent variable.[6] These models contain sector dummies for post and rail. Model IV uses the cross-sector average per country as the dependent variable. All models include the initial value of the index of public entrepreneurship (IPEr) in 1980. We also control for other possible determinants of privatization discussed in the literature. Since the number of observations is small, we only include one control variable per model. Table 5.9 contains those control variables that reach statistical significance. This applies only for union density and the initial size of IPEr. Strong unions have in fact inhibited privatization of the network-based infrastructure sectors. In addition, Figure 5.3 shows the impact of the index of constitutional barriers for a set of important control variables. The operationalization of all variables can be found in the appendix (Table A.2).

The findings related to the index of constitutional barriers are compelling as they clearly demonstrate that high constitutional barriers slow down the privatization of public utilities. The higher the index of constitutional barriers, the higher is the public involvement in the public utility sectors. Irrespective

---

[5] See Chapter 4 for details on the measurement.
[6] Railway services in Japan and Australia as well as postal services in Italy could not be included in the analysis since several companies were responsible for service provision.

Determinants of Privatization: Empirical Findings

Table 5.9. The impact of constitutional barriers on privatization

Dependent variable: public involvement

Independent variables	(I)	(II)	(III)	(IV)
Constitutional framework	1.16***	1.56***	1.28***	1.69***
	0.334	0.371	0.407	0.417
Union density	–	0.074**	–	0.083**
		0.034		0.039
Initial size of public entrepreneurship	19.78***	18.25***	21.13***	18.27***
	3.35	3.31	5.72	5.38
Adj. R^2	0.586	0.613	0.489	0.576
N	57	57	57	20

Notes: (clustered) standard errors in parentheses; *** $p<0.01$, ** $p<0.05$, * $p<0.1$

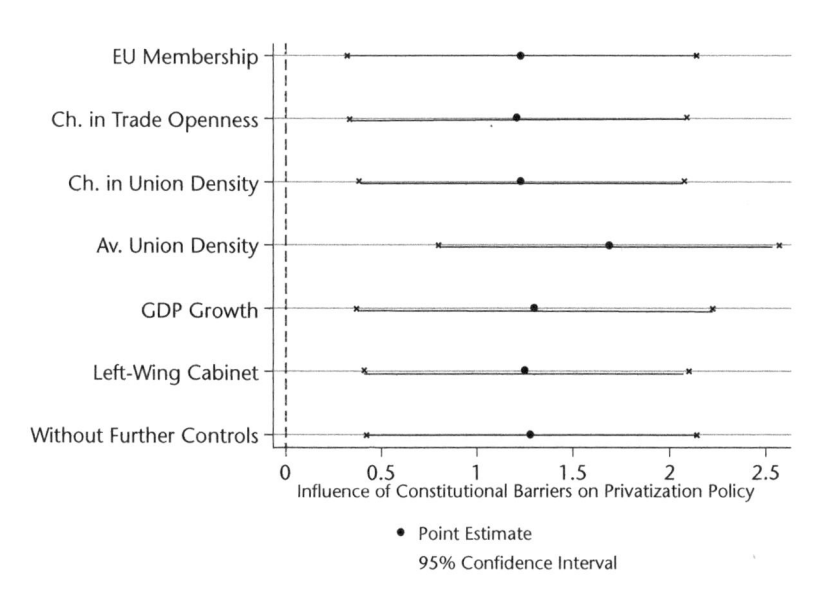

Figure 5.3. The impact of constitutional barriers contingent upon varying control variables

of the controls used, the point estimation of the coefficient is positive and significantly different from 0 at the 5 percent level (Figure 5.3). With regard to the control variables, we find that the initial size of public entrepreneurship is a key variable. This is particularly notable since this variable has not been taken into account by previous research due to lacking data on the size of the public enterprise sector. The positive coefficient indicates that state involvement is higher in countries that already had a big public enterprise sector at the beginning of the period of examination.

Partisan Politics and Privatization Policies

Apart from institutional effects, our major research interest focuses on the impact of political parties on privatization. As we have seen in Chapter 3, the empirical findings of the extant literature are inconclusive. While several studies conclude that partisan effects have disappeared over time, other inquiries still find evidence supportive of classic partisan theory. We argue that the contradictory findings are closely related to inappropriate estimation techniques. More specifically, we contend that the standard panel design might not be the most appropriate estimation strategy when the influence of political parties is the variable of theoretical interest. Standard panel designs typically focus on short-term changes within countries. However, the party composition of governments typically does not change on a yearly basis but usually at elections. Moreover, parties often need time to develop and implement substantive policies and therefore to change policies according to their preferences. That makes it less likely for partisan variables to become statistically significant in panel regressions based on country years.

Instead, we propose to adjust the methodological framework to the political cycle and suggest a simple and straightforward alternative which in our view is more appropriate for examining the influence of partisan politics on public policy. We use cabinets as units of analysis instead of country years as a more appropriate empirical translation of partisan theory which predicts that governments take decisions during their incumbency and change policies according to their preferences (see for a detailed discussion Schmitt 2015). We define a government as a 'cabinet with the same party composition (even if there are new elections or the prime minister changes but is of the same party)' (Boix 1997: 483). Nonetheless, a cabinet formed by the same parties as the last one is still counted as a new cabinet if the cabinet shares held by the coalition partners change. To give an example: the German coalition of Christian democrats and liberals under Chancellor Helmut Kohl lasted from 1982 to 1998. As the cabinet shares held by the coalition partners changed after each election, however, we count four cabinets (Obinger et al. 2014).

For our analysis we exclude all cabinets that have been in power for less than one year since short-term cabinets such as caretaker governments are typically unable to launch major privatization programmes. The starting and end point of each government is based on the years in which the cabinet has been in power after a period of six months. For example, if a cabinet took office in May 1985, the starting year is 1985. However, if a cabinet took power in September 1985, the starting year would be 1986. If the year in which the cabinet comes to power is equal to the year of cabinet change or government break-down, the case drops out of the sample. Following this coding procedure, we end up with 111 cabinets in our twenty countries.

Determinants of Privatization: Empirical Findings

Our dependent variable in the regression analysis is the change of the IPE (Revenue and Employment Index) which is measured by the difference between the index value in the first and the last year of a particular cabinet. Note that positive values therefore indicate privatization.

To capture partisan effects on privatization, we employ two different measures. First, we use the cabinet seats held by left (social democratic and communist) and conservative parties. Second, we use data measuring the ideological position of the government on a left–right scale. These data derive from Döring and Manow (2011). The left–right position of each party in government is weighted by the seats of that party in parliament in relation to the total number of parliamentary seats held by cabinet parties. Since we rely on cabinets as units of observations, we have to control for cabinet duration. In this respect, we assume that cabinet longevity is positively associated with privatization intensity as stable governments are in a better position to launch comprehensive privatization programmes.

With the exception of party ideology, cabinet composition, cabinet duration, and the initial size of the public enterprise sector, all independent variables refer to the first half of the cabinet period in order to avoid endogeneity problems. For example, for a cabinet in office from 1990 to 1996, the values of the independent variables reflect averages of the years 1990 to 1993. Details on the variables and their measurement can be found in the appendix (Table A.2).

The empirical findings reported in Table 5.10 strongly corroborate classic partisan theory. Left governments have privatized less than right-wing cabinets irrespective of whether the Employment or Revenue Index is considered. In all four models (I to IV) the coefficient shows the theoretically expected sign and is statistically significant at least at the 10 per cent level. This finding is supported by models V and VI which examine whether a government's ideological orientation on a left–right scale has influenced privatization efforts. Since high values of this variable reflect a pronounced pro-market orientation, the positive and statistically significant coefficient indicates that right-wing cabinets pushed the divesture of state-owned enterprises more extensively than their left competitors.

In terms of the control variables, we find the expected positive impact of cabinet longevity on privatization. Strong and stable governments apparently are better able to launch larger and thus potentially conflictive privatization programmes than short-lived cabinets.

Fiscal problem pressure turns out as an important trigger of public sector restructuring. The level of public debt is consistently positive but statistically insignificant. However, countries with high budget deficits in the run up to the enforcement of the Treaty of Maastricht launched privatization programmes in an effort to meet the deficit criterion enshrined in this Treaty. This effect is stable and statistically significant across all models.

Table 5.10. Partisan impacts on privatization

Dependent variable: privatization

Independent variables	(I) IPEr	(II) IPEe	(III) IPEr	(IV) IPEe	(V) IPEr	(VI) IPEe
Left-wing cabinet	−0.634** (0.278)	−240** (0.107)	–	–	–	–
Conservative cabinet	–	–	0.662** (0.274)	0.193* (0.109)	–	–
Ideological position	–	–	–	–	0.173** (0.082)	0.061* (0.033)
Maastricht	0.488** (0.218)	0.194** (0.078)	0.461** (0.212)	0.180** (0.072)	0.525** (0.215)	0.205** (0.081)
Debt	0.003 (0.002)	0.0002 (0.0007)	0.003 (0.002)	0.001 (0.001)	0.003 (0.003)	0.0003 (0.0008)
GDP per capita (log.)	−1.09** (0.483)	−0.075 (0.124)	−1.10** (0.428)	−0.070 (0.114)	−1.09** (0.436)	−0.065 (0.118)
GDP growth	−0.069 (0.050)	−0.019 (0.015)	−0.010** (0.043)	−0.029* (0.016)	−0.070 (0.049)	−0.020 (0.015)
Trade openness	0.006 (0.004)	0.002 (0.002)	0.008** (0.004)	0.002 (0.002)	0.008* (0.004)	0.002 (0.002)
Union density	−0.010** (0.005)	−0.002 (0.002)	−0.010** (0.005)	−0.002 (0.002)	−0.010** (0.005)	−0.002 (0.002)
Years in power	0.144* (0.079)	0.094*** (0.032)	0.130 (0.079)	0.091*** (0.032)	0.143* (0.077)	0.094*** (0.031)
Initial size of public entrepreneurship	0.081** (0.039)	0.134*** (0.078)	0.082** (0.040)	0.146*** (0.040)	0.089** (0.040)	0.147 (0.039)
F	4.01***	2.19**	3.41***	2.54**	4.15***	2.55**
N	111	111	111	111	111	111

Notes: clustered standard errors in parentheses; *** $p<0.01$, ** $p<0.05$, * $p<0.1$.

Union density is negative in all models but only statistically significant for the IPEr. Similar to left parties, union strength has impeded the divesture of public enterprises. The initial size of the public enterprise sector is a further important variable in explaining privatization intensity. The bigger the initial size of public entrepreneurship the more governments relied on privatization. The coefficients of economic growth and GDP per capita are consistently negative and statistically significant in several models. This means that privatization activities were accelerated by low economic growth but were less comprehensive in richer countries. Finally, we find evidence that economic globalization is a trigger of privatization. The openness of the economy to trade is positive in all models and even statistically significant in two specifications.

In a final step, we now study interactions between political parties and institutions since theory predicts that the room to manoeuvre for political actors is conditioned by the institutional setting (Schmidt 1996). The extent to which political actors can enforce their preferences should be influenced by

Table 5.11. Interaction effects of parties and institutions on privatization

Dependent variable: privatization (using IPEr)

Independent variables	(I)	(II)	(III)
Left-leaning cabinet	−0.617** (0.251)		
Conservative cabinet		0.567** (0.259)	
Ideological position			0.187** (0.077)
Constitutional barriers	0.023 (0.058)	0.010 (0.075)	0.047 (0.053)
Constitutional barriers *Partisan variables	0.172* (0.093)	−0.370* (0.224)	−0.067** (0.032)
F	3.36***	3.20***	4.02***
N	111	111	111

Notes: clustered standard errors in parentheses; *** p<0.01, ** p<0.05, * p<0.1; results for control variables are suppressed to conserve space

the national institutional environment. In the second section of this chapter we argued and provided evidence that the constitutional framework is an important institutional factor when it comes to the privatization of public utilities. Now we examine whether the impact of the partisan complexion of government on privatization is conditioned by constitutional barriers. Partisan impacts are again measured by cabinet shares and the ideological positions of governments on a left–right scale, whereas our index of constitutional barriers captures a government's capacity to act. Both variables were mean centred before constructing the interaction variable. Table 5.11 summarizes the empirical results for the overall Revenue Index. Model I uses the cabinet shares of leftist parties, Model II relies on the cabinet shares of conservative parties, while Model III tests the ideological orientation of governments.[7]

The findings are very intriguing and strongly support theoretical reasoning on how institutions work. The interaction variables are statistically significant in all three models. In Model I, the positive interaction coefficient suggests that constitutional barriers compensate the negative effect of left-wing parties on privatization. Left governments operating in a permissive institutional context are more reluctant to stand against privatization than left cabinets in countries with high barriers. It seems that the necessity for left parties to oppose privatization is relatively low in countries with high constitutional barriers. In contrast, in Model II, the interaction variable shows a negative sign. Conservative parties confronted with high constitutional barriers are not

---

[7] The effects of the control variables strongly mirror the findings in Table 5.10 and are therefore suppressed to conserve space. Globalization, low economic growth, cabinet stability, budget deficits, and a big sector are driving factors of privatization, whereas economic affluence and strong unions impede the divestue of state-owned enterprises.

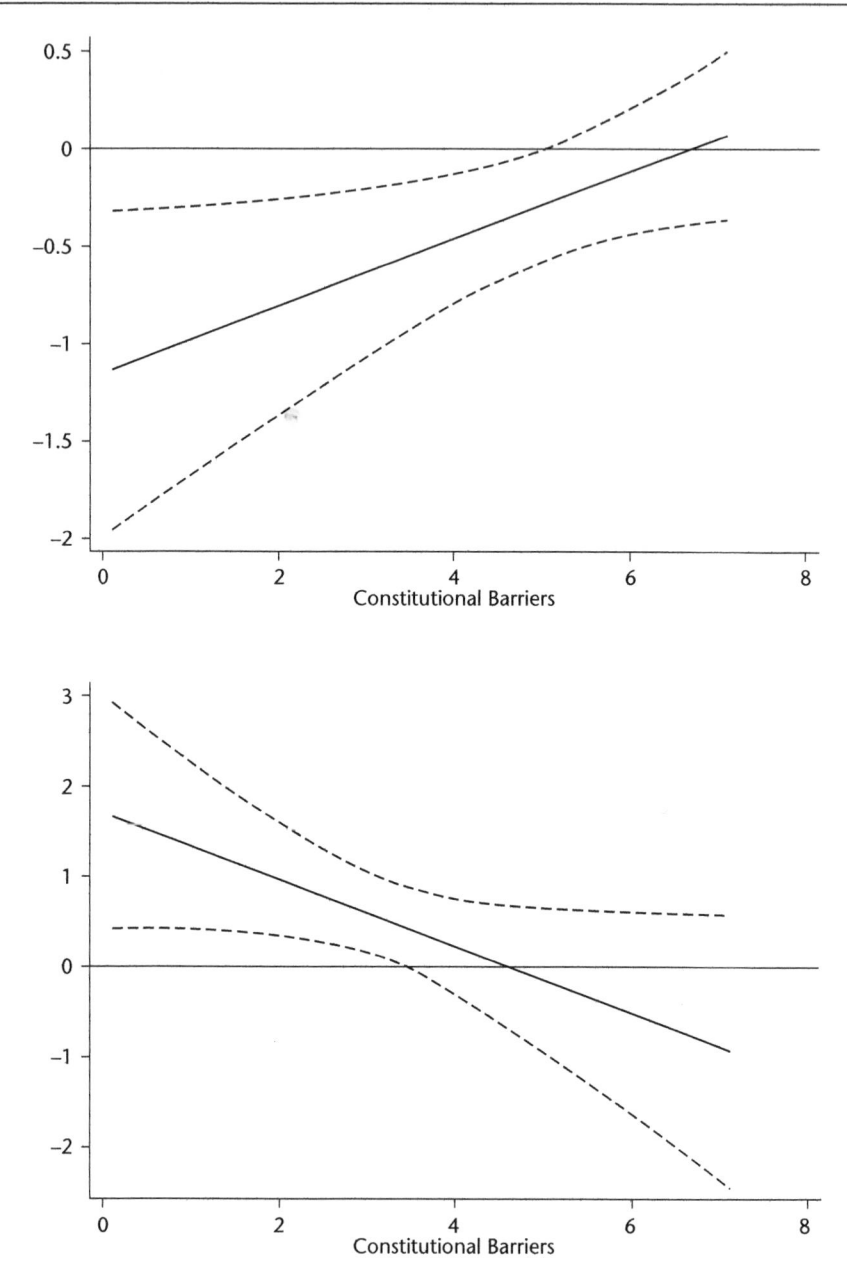

Figure 5.4. Marginal effects of left (top) and conservative (bottom) cabinets

Determinants of Privatization: Empirical Findings

able to launch privatization programmes to the same extent as conservative parties in settings characterized by low constitutional barriers. Constitutional rigidities related to public utilities therefore constrain conservative parties in their efforts to privatize public enterprises. Model III replicates this finding for government ideology. The higher the number of constitutional barriers the smaller is the positive impact of right-wing parties on privatization.

The conditional effects are further illustrated by the marginal effect plots in Figure 5.4. It is shown that the effect of left cabinets on privatization is negative and statistically significant only in those countries where the value for constitutional barriers is lower than about 5. In countries such as Germany and Spain with constitutional barriers above 5 the reluctance of left cabinets against privatization is weaker since the institutions assume part of the task. Conservative cabinets privatize public enterprises to a greater extent only under favourable institutional conditions. When the constitutional barriers are equal to about 3.5, i.e. slightly above the mean (mean = 3.106) the positive effect on privatization is no longer statistically significant.

The Diffusion of Privatization Policies

In Chapter 3, we argued that privatization policies have diffused across countries. For example, neighbouring countries and countries sharing strong economic relationships should influence each other when implementing privatization programmes. To test policy diffusion we rely on spatial econometrics. In spatial regression models interdependencies between countries can be modelled by including a spatial term as a regressor (spatial lag model) (Anselin 2003). The general spatio-temporal autoregressive model can be expressed as follows:

$$y = \rho \, W \, y + \varphi \, L \, y + \phi \, M \, y + \beta \, X + \epsilon$$

where y is the index of public entrepreneurship (see above). ρ and φ are spatial autoregressive coefficients. Wy and Ly are weighting averages of the dependent variable (spatial lag). The spatial weight matrix W reflects the relative connectivity of each sector in each country i to every other sector in every other country at time t. The effect on a focal sector in a focal country at time t is then a weighted sum of outcomes across countries (Lee and Strang 2006). L is the weighting matrix capturing cross-sector diffusion. The effect on a focal sector in a focal country at time t is then a weighted sum of outcomes across the other two sectors of that focal country. ϕ denotes the temporal autoregressive coefficient and M an NT×NT matrix to create the first order temporal lag (those on the minor diagonal). X is a set of exogenous right-hand side variables.

Before analysing different diffusion mechanisms, we need to examine whether there is spatial association in the dependent variable. Our dependent variable is the revenue-based index of public entrepreneurship (IPEr).[8] Moran's I as well as Geary's C indicate spatial correlation for the dependent variables. Furthermore, the local indicators for spatial association show that the spatial correlation is not caused by a single value.

True spatial interdependence has to be carefully distinguished from other sources of spatial association as spatial patterns in the dependent variable might also be caused by common shocks or trends or unobserved spatial heterogeneity. The only possibility for disentangling spatial dependence from its alternatives is to model it and include appropriate right-hand side variables (Plümper and Neumayer 2010: 215). A failure to account for such alternatives will bias the spatial lag coefficient. To control for common shocks, we added time dummies. Furthermore, a lagged dependent variable captures common trends and temporal dynamics. A lagged dependent variable has the disadvantage of accounting for the largest part of the variance in the dependent variable and of absorbing the explanatory power of the other substantial right-hand variables. However, the focus is on guaranteeing reliable results for the spatial lags. This procedure is a very conservative test strategy for the hypotheses on spatial interdependencies. To cope with the unobserved spatial heterogeneity country fixed effect models are estimated. The fixed effect variables also help to control for alternative sources of spatial patterns in the dependent variable. Spatial diagnostic tests on the residuals of the non-spatial model using OLS give further information about the nature of the spatial association. The Robust Lagrange Multiplier Test against the spatial lag or spatial error alternative indicates whether the spatial association is caused by unobserved factors. The results clearly support the spatial lag alternatives (Anselin et al. 1996; Franzese and Hays 2007, 2008).

We use four different weighting matrices to test whether learning, emulation, or competition matters for privatization policy. First, privatization policy is weighted by the *inverse distance between the capitals* to capture whether neighbouring countries influence each other. Second, weighting the public entrepreneurship with the sum of exports and imports between two countries as a percentage of the *total trade volume* enables checking whether trading partners adopt similar policies. Third, the correlation between the trade volume of each pair of countries to all other trade partners is used to measure the extent of bilateral *trade competition*. Two countries score high if they both have similar trading partners (i.e. compete for similar markets) and even if they do not trade much with each other. With the last weighting matrix we test

---

[8] To keep the presentation of our results parsimonious, we only display the maximum likelihood estimations for the IPEr.

Determinants of Privatization: Empirical Findings

whether privatization policy is influenced by horizontal diffusion among member countries of the European Union. The cells of the respective weighting matrix equal 1 if two countries both belong to the European Union in a respective year and 0 otherwise. All weighting matrices are row standardized so that each row adds up to a total of 1. Details on the measurement of all variables can be found in the appendix (Table A.2).

Table 5.12 reports the empirical findings which strongly suggest that privatization has diffused across the OECD world. Diffusion is driven by trade relations and geographical proximity rather than by the competition for markets and the European Union. Neighbouring countries and countries that are strongly economically linked influence each other and move in the same direction. This can be seen from the fact that the coefficients of the spatial lags related to geographical proximity and the intensity of trade relations are positive and statistically significant. Countries apparently tend to privatize when trading partners or countries that are geographically close to them do so. It is therefore the policy trend amongst geographically and economically related countries that drive forward the diffusion of

Table 5.12. The diffusion of privatization policy

Dependent variable: Index of Public Entrepreneurship (IPEr)

Independent variables	(I) Trade relations	(II) Geographical proximity	(III) Economic competition	(IV) EU: horizontal diffusion
$IPEr_{t-1}$	0.848***	0.0848***	0.853***	0.852***
	(0.0185)	(0.0186)	(0.0187)	(0.0188)
Trade openness	−0.00982***	−0.00957***	−0.0114***	−0.0113***
	(0.00320)	(0.00325)	(0.00308)	(0.00326)
GDP per capita (log.)	0.297	0.311	0.0526	0.0415
	(0.331)	(0.338)	(0.301)	(0.354)
GDP growth	0.00285	0.00315	0.00538	0.00520
	(0.0117)	(0.0117)	(0.0116)	(0.0118)
Debt	−0.00330**	−0.00318**	−0.00464***	−0.00463***
	(0.00149)	(0.00155)	(0.00127)	(0.00159)
Political institutions	0.299	0.269	0.293	0.281
	(0.389)	(0.389)	(0.391)	(0.391)
EU membership	−0.0697	−0.0649	−0.0503	−0.0494
	(0.0954)	(0.0952)	(0.0954)	(0.0964)
Leftist government	0.00146**	0.00151***	0.00143**	0.00137**
	(0.000579)	(0.000583)	(0.000586)	(0.000580)
Union density	0.0112*	0.0116*	0.0103*	0.0106*
	(0.00625)	(0.00626)	(0.00627)	(0.00626)
Spatial lag	0.0934*	0.0895*	0.0138	0.0138
	(0.0505)	(0.0499)	(0.0201)	(0.0583)
Wald Chi	23324.17***	24344.03***	25488.82***	24946.13***
N	481	481	481	481

Notes: the fixed effects are suppressed to conserve space; standard errors in parentheses; *** z, p<0.01, ** z, p<0.05, * z, p<0.1

privatization policy. Strikingly, the coefficient of the spatial lag capturing competition between countries turns out to be statistically insignificant. Countries competing for the same markets thus do not necessarily implement the same privatization policies. There is also no evidence that horizontal diffusion among EU members plays a major role when it comes to privatization. The influence of the EU on privatization policies is vertical in nature rather than horizontal. Schmitt (2013), for example, shows that EU directives clearly foster the privatization of postal services but rather decelerate the privatization process in the railways sector.

With regard to the control variables, we find a consistent negative effect for trade openness. Increasing the openness of the economy puts pressure on governments to decrease the involvement of the state in the national economy. Moreover, privatization is stimulated by high levels of public debt. Finally, strong left-wing parties and trade unions inhibit a strong retreat of the state from entrepreneurial activities. All other control variables turn out to be statistically insignificant.

Summary

When summarizing the main results of this chapter, the following empirical findings stand out. First, the evidence for convergence is mixed. Even though most of the countries retreated from entrepreneurial activities, public involvement in the economy remains high in Nordic countries.

Second, the partisanship of political actors still matters in times of economically integrated markets. In almost all models it turns out that left governments more reluctantly privatize than their conservative counterparts. Furthermore, labour unions as the main opponents against privatization often are a successfully countervailing force. This especially applies for the network-based utility sectors where labour unions are traditionally strong and very well organized.

Third, political institutions only are relevant for privatization when looking at the policy-specific institutional environment. Popular indices that include general political institutions such as federalism and bicameralism neither facilitate nor inhibit privatizations. In contrast, when looking at constitutional barriers as policy-specific institutions for privatization we find strong evidence that these institutional characteristics effectively constrain the possibilities for governments to implement privatization programmes.

Fourth, privatization is fuelled by empty public coffers. Governments faced with high public debt use privatization to raise revenues in order to attenuate the fiscal pressure.

Regarding international factors, we find that privatization tends to be greatest in countries highly involved in the global economy. Economic integration seems to put pressure on governments to reduce the public intrusion in economic affairs.

And last, privatization is not only a national phenomenon. Interdependencies between countries influence the possibilities and choices countries perceive and have. Countries privatize when economically related countries and closely located countries do so.

6

Conclusion and Outlook

This concluding chapter briefly summarizes the findings of this book, provides an overview of the development of public entrepreneurship in the wake of the recent economic and financial crisis, and speculates on the future role of the state as an entrepreneur.

Public Entrepreneurship in the Long Run

Public enterprises, notably public utilities, played an important role in economic and social policy during the first three decades after the Second World War. State-owned enterprises, however, have a much longer history. Examples are state monopolies such as salt, tobacco, and sugar which were used to raise revenues for the Crown. Moreover, the state was from early on involved in the mining and the munitions industries. The formation and proliferation of modern public enterprises commenced in the second half of the 19th century but was, initially, mainly restricted to the local level. Key aspects of public provision of goods and services were efforts to protect citizens from the negative repercussions of industrialization and urbanization. Nation-state building, technological change, military interests, and efforts to accelerate economic development led to the build-up of public infrastructures in sectors such as transportation, telecommunications, energy, and postal services at the national level. Public enterprises in these sectors were designed to help to forge and control national territories, strengthen military defence, and promote industrialization. Beyond public utilities, governments increasingly became engaged in industrial companies, mining, and the oil business. Military considerations often were crucial in this respect. This is evident from state involvement in steelworks, shipyards, the munitions and chemicals industries, or in engineering. Both world wars and the Great Depression were important turning points in terms of state interference in economic and social affairs. The massive expansion of state intervention that occurred during wartime and economic crisis under governments of all political complexions was only gradually reversed in the aftermath of military conflict. In addition, both world wars strengthened the fiscal and administrative powers of the state and governments gained experience in managing the economy during wartime.

The repercussions of mass warfare brought about a further boost to public ownership as many European countries suffered from massive war-related destruction, especially after the Second World War, when large parts of the infrastructure and many production sites were destroyed by acts of war. Economic reconstruction in war-torn nations often required massive state aid given the adverse and sometimes disastrous economic conditions of the immediate post-war years. Against the backdrop of economic and political turbulence, governments mostly responded pragmatically rather than ideologically. The bitter lessons of economic depression and total war had a long-term impact on individual and collective preferences and led to a shift toward state intervention in most advanced democracies during the so-called *trente glorieuses*.

One element of the emerging Keynesian post-war compromise was the notion that public enterprises could and should provide transport, postal, and telecommunications services, electricity and gas supplies, and a broad range of local services. Public provision of these goods and services also aimed at fulfilling important social welfare functions so that public utilities complemented the activities of the core welfare state. Moreover, albeit to varying degrees, new state-owned companies emerged in manufacturing, heavy industry, and the finance sector. It was only after the Second World War that the political left utilized state-owned enterprises for economic and social planning on a major scale. However, as the historical origins of public enterprises were anything but an exclusively leftist preserve, the political manipulation of SOEs in the post-war period was a cross-party phenomenon. Christian democrats in Italy or conservative policy makers in Greece, just to name a few examples, repeatedly intervened in commercial decisions or utilized SOEs for allocating jobs to party members. The resulting overstaffing of companies, patronage politics, and the politically mandated imposition of strategic objectives on companies other than profit maximization led to growing inefficiencies at the firm level. However, the exceptional rate of economic growth and the relative closure of Western economies in the wake of the Second World War cushioned the structural problems of state-owned enterprises for almost three decades.

However, once the economic boom period related to economic reconstruction abated and the oil shocks of the 1970s hit the Western democracies, the poor performance and inefficiencies of many public companies became apparent and raised increasing concerns. The oil shocks were just one of a number of factors impelling the late 20th-century transformation of the state-owned enterprise sector. Apart from stagflation, massive technological change, growing public debt, globalization, the formation of the EMU, and the spread of neo-liberal ideas, not least reinforced by the collapse of the command economies in Eastern Europe, have also accelerated public sector restructuring. Public ownership of firms and, more generally, excessive state intervention in economic affairs were increasingly seen as the root cause of the poor economic performance of Western economies. In consequence, the privatization of state-owned firms moved to the top of national political agendas. Starting in the English-speaking world in the early 1980s, governments in Western democracies have sold off public enterprises to an unprecedented extent. However, both the timing and the scope of privatization activities differed considerably across countries.

Based on a new database which includes approximately 1,500 public enterprises operating at the national level in twenty countries and relying on a two-dimensional conceptualization of privatization, we commenced our empirical analysis by describing the scope of privatization activities over the last thirty years. According to our data the size of the public enterprise sector at the national level differed widely across countries in 1980. In terms of national privatization trajectories, our findings point to more heterogeneous developments than expected. Despite a general trend towards privatization across the OECD world with Norway as a spectacular outlier, we have identified a considerable variation across countries and sectors in terms of the chronology and the extent of privatizations implemented at the national level. While governments in the English-speaking countries massively withdrew from entrepreneurial activities, state intrusion in economic and commercial affairs has remained substantially greater in Scandinavia. Furthermore, it turned out that all these nations maintained particular strategic sectors.

When accounting for these cross-national differences, we identified a combination of national and international factors shaping national privatization pathways. According to our empirical findings economic globalization and fiscal problem pressure were important triggers of privatization. Furthermore, international interdependencies clearly influenced privatization activities. Countries jumped onto the privatization bandwagon when economically or geographically closely related countries started to divest public enterprises. With regard to domestic determinants, we have shown that the partisan complexion of government is important for privatization, as right-wing parties were more inclined to sell off SOEs than left parties. Moreover, the privatization of public utilities was shaped by constitutional provisions which constrained the room to manoeuvre of governments seeking to restructure their public infrastructure sectors. Together with legal researchers, we developed a new index which is important for understanding cross-national differences in the timing and scope of public utility privatization.

Conclusion and Outlook

However, the overall trend favouring the privatization of public enterprises from the 1980s onwards should not obscure the fact that some sectors witnessed a transformation rather than a retreat of state intervention. A transformation of state activities is most evident in the public utility sectors: while these services were initially provided privately, later subjected to public regulation and, ultimately, nationalized in all OECD countries with the notable exception of the U.S., public utility providers have been formally privatized and/or sold off over the past three decades. A crucial precondition of formal and material privatization was market liberalization (Holzinger and Schmidt 2015). However, the opening of markets and the subsequent privatization of the public incumbents went along with an expansion of state regulation that was typically delegated to newly established regulatory agencies (RAs). These institutions spread massively over the past three decades (Vogel 1998; Gilardi 2005; Jordana et al. 2011). This well-documented development has been described as 'transformation from the positive to the regulatory state' (Majone 1994), the 'global diffusion of regulatory capitalism' (Levi-Faur 2005), or summarized by the slogan 'freer markets, more rules' (Vogel 1998).

Figure 6.1 graphically illustrates this transformation for the countries examined in this volume. The solid line (left axis) denotes an index of product market regulation in six non-manufacturing sectors (Conway and Nicoletti 2006), ranging from 0 (very competitive market) to 6 (very restrictive market). The dotted line (right axis) illustrates the accumulated number of RAs in these sectors. While markets became more competitive over time, the rapid proliferation of RAs suggests that the pronounced market liberalization from the 1990s onwards was paralleled by more regulation.

What we thus observe in the utility sectors is a convergence towards the U.S. regulatory model that prevailed throughout the 20th century and, seen from a longer historical perspective, the recurrence of the 19th century's mode of governance with private firms as the main service providers and government bodies as regulators. Beneath this common trend, however, the national practice of liberalization and re-regulation differed markedly across countries (Vogel 1998).

In contrast to the utility sectors, there was a massive retreat of the state in manufacturing. Industrial companies where governments are majority shareholders or which are even operated by the state itself (e.g. a ministry) are nowadays extremely rare. Minority shareholding is more common but mainly restricted to fiscally or strategically relevant sectors such as the oil business or the aviation and space industry. Public companies in the financial sector have also experienced a major decline since the 1990s. However, privatization activities in this sector were brutally stopped with the onset of the global credit crunch.

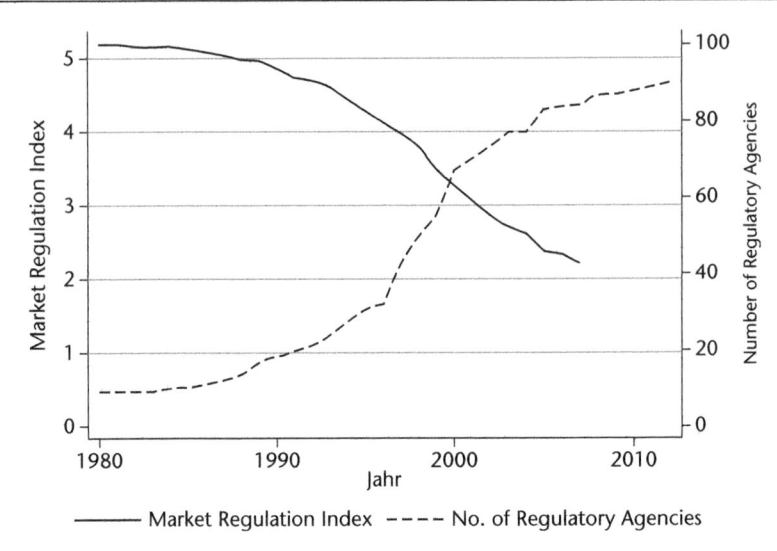

Political Economy of Privatization in Rich Democracies

Figure 6.1. Product market liberalization and the spread of regulatory agencies since 1980

Notes: national regulation authorities in the twenty OECD countries featuring in our sample plus the United States

Source: market regulation index: Conway and Nicoletti (2006); RAs: own compilation based on national reports, OECD, and EU documents

The Impact of the Financial Crisis

Our empirical analysis ended with the advent of the global economic crisis. While the past three decades were mainly characterized by a roll-back and restructuring of the public enterprise sector, the role of the state as entrepreneur has been challenged by the global financial crisis and its aftershocks. Like all previous emergencies in history, the recent economic slump witnessed company bail-outs on a massive scale.

The financial crisis led to the worst global recession since the Second World War (IMF 2009). The Great Recession began with the contraction of the U.S. economy in December 2007 and eventually ended in September 2009. In the course of the crisis, the OECD countries examined in this book expended enormous efforts to stabilize their staggering economies and financial sectors in particular. According to our calculations, the total financial volume of nationalizations amounted to an impressive 1.083 trillion US dollars between 2008 and 2012. About 75 per cent thereof was realized during the recession years 2008 and 2009. Table 6.1 lists the nationalization volumes by country. The second column reports the total value of nationalizations in million US dollars (current values) and the third column the respective per capita values in US dollars. The fourth column represents the nationalization

Conclusion and Outlook

Table 6.1. Nationalization volumes by country, 2008–12

Country	Total (million US dollars)	Per capita (US dollars)	As a pct. of average GDP	Rank
Australia	0	0	0.00	20
Austria	9,017	1,078	2.24	9
Belgium	40,278	3,688	7.96	3
Canada	0	0	0.00	20
Denmark	5,468	986	1.66	12
Finland	1,384	258	0.56	15
France	33,395	531	1.20	14
Germany	48,200	589	1.36	13
Greece	33,737	3,026	11.71	2
Ireland	51,341	11,292	22.56	1
Italy	8,196	136	0.39	16
Japan	4,154	33	0.08	18
Netherlands	57,778	3,479	6.71	4
New Zealand	467	107	0.33	17
Norway	8,220	1,680	1.86	11
Portugal	9,934	941	4.45	7
Spain	81,436	1,771	5.87	5
Sweden	325	35	0.07	19
Switzerland	11,060	1,421	2.09	10
United Kingdom	109,342	1,765	4.51	6
United States	569,281	1,842	3.76	8

Notes: own calculations based on various public sources such as government shareholding reports and company annual reports

volume as a percentage of average GDP, while the fifth column shows the corresponding rank.

In absolute terms, the U.S. excelled all other countries in terms of the volume of nationalization. The U.S. government's capital purchase programme, established in February 2009, provided back-up capital to more than 700 financial institutions (Glasserman and Wang 2011) and reached a volume of 179 billion US dollars. Beyond the capital purchase programme, AIG received almost 70 billion US dollars, whereas Fannie Mae and Freddy Mac were together supported with 187 billion US dollars. The only prominent nationalization outside the financial sector was the 60 per cent shareholding in General Motors acquired in 2009, worth 48.87 billion US dollars. In relative terms (i.e. as a percentage of GDP), three small countries, namely Ireland, Greece, and Belgium, were forced by the crisis into the largest nationalization programmes. Ireland's bank recapitalization scheme became effective in February 2009 and involved, as a first step, bail-outs equivalent to 3.5 billion euros of the Allied Irish Banks (AIB) and Bank of Ireland Group. Up until 2012, AIB had received back-up capital of no less than 13.3 billion euros. Australia and Canada were the only countries in the sample which did not resort to major nationalizations.

The data clearly indicate that the nationalization wave during and in the aftermath of the Great Recession was triggered by the financial crisis and the related urgent need for a recapitalization of the financial sector. No less than 93 per cent of public money was assigned to the financial sector. In most instances, capital assistance was provided in terms of common tier 1 capital (64 per cent) or additional tier 1 capital (8 per cent). Capital assistance was frequently granted by government-related bodies that were created for the special purpose of financial market stabilization (like Germany's *SoFFin-Sonderfonds Finanzmarktstabilisierung*) rather than provided from the ordinary budget. Also note that many financial institutions that were either forced to participate in state recapitalization programmes or participated voluntarily began to redeem government shares soon after economic recovery. For example, the *Banques Populaires Caisses d'Epargne* (France) quickly repaid its capital assistance of about 5 billion euros until the end of 2011. Most governments concentrated on 'rescuing' so-called system-relevant financial institutions that were threatened in their existence by the crisis in order to keep the financial system as a whole alive. If possible, policy makers abstained from obtaining a majority of the company in question and in no way tried to exercise control on corporate policies except for the regulation of management salaries. This is also reflected in the fact that capital assistance was provided in terms of nonvoting preferred stock (additional tier 1 capital) that will phase out with the implementation of Basel III.

While national governments spent more than 1 trillion US dollars during and after the financial crisis with a view to stabilizing the world financial system, the process of privatization was not discontinued. Table 6.2 shows the privatization revenues for the fourteen EU countries included in our sample accrued over the 2008–13 period, i.e. after the outbreak of the Great Recession. Revenues are expressed in million US dollars (current values) and taken from the Privatization Barometer database.

In sum, 281.2 billion US dollars was generated from privatizations over this period. Annual revenues amounted to 47 billion US dollars on average and varied from 22 billion US dollars in 2011 to more than 73 billion US dollars in 2008. Moreover, Table 6.2 illustrates a substantial variation both across and within countries. Austria brings up the rear, privatizing only three SOEs. The most prominent example was the Hypo Group Alpe Adria Bank (Austrian subsidiary) in 2013, involving a volume of 85 million US dollars. Note that Hypo Group Alpe Adria had been renationalized for a symbolic price of 4 euros in 2009.[1] France, by contrast, is in the privatization vanguard as the country

---

[1] The Hypo Group Alpe Adria Bank is an example of how great the costs of rescue operations may become in the long run. To date (February 2015), Austrian taxpayers have had to cover the 5.5

Table 6.2. Privatization revenues of fourteen EU countries, 2008–13

Country/year	2008	2009	2010	2011	2012	2013	Sum (2008–13)
Austria	1	0	0	14	0	85	99
Belgium	0	6	0	20	0	5.664	5.690
Denmark	435	148	524	163	76	2.008	3.354
Finland	0	329	306	0	195	340	1.170
France	28.841	16.351	13.964	2.621	566	5.543	67.887
Germany	10.178	6.815	5.544	0	2.466	4.074	29.076
Greece	4.984	2.840	0	2.800	0	11.190	21.815
Ireland	707	0	0	6.889	9.231	1.738	18.565
Italy	1.881	16	3.435	518	5.103	1	10.955
Netherlands	484	15.122	1.188	0	40	0	16.834
Portugal	3.370	0	1.183	3.515	11.035	5.445	24.549
Spain	0	0	1.325	845	1.221	3.861	7.252
Sweden	20.673	277	299	3.026	1.180	7.480	32.935
United Kingdom	1.787	11.115	6.787	1.095	3.965	16.277	41.026
Sum	73.341	53.019	34.555	21.506	35.078	63.704	281.203

Notes: privatization revenues are given in million US dollars (current values)

Data source: Privatization Barometer (<http://www.privatizationbarometer.net>)

has not only raised the highest revenues, but also realized forty privatization deals. The treasury collected roughly 68 billion US dollars, mostly in the immediate post-crisis period. France also implemented the largest single privatization deal of the period. The merger of Gaz de France with Suez in 2008 involved a 21 billion US dollar sale of a 44.1 per cent share of Gaz de France by public offer.

Figure 6.2 displays the privatization revenues accrued over the 2008–13 period as a percentage of GDP. Three out of the four countries that had to resort to the Euro Bailout Fund are to be found in the top group, namely Ireland, Portugal, and Greece. By contrast, Spain launched twenty-three relatively small privatizations over the 2008–13 period which only amounted to 0.08 per cent of GDP. Sweden, which is also located in the top group, privatized thirty-one state-owned enterprises and raised revenues equivalent to 1.37 per cent of GDP. Sweden's largest single privatization deal was the public sale of Vin & Spirit AB in 2008 (8.9 billion US dollars).

For the remaining six non-EU countries included in our book we do not have detailed privatization data at our disposal for the years after 2007. However, taking a glance at worldwide privatization revenues based on data collected by the Privatization Barometer shows that the privatization trend also continues elsewhere: during the period from 2008 to 2013, the world's

billion euros shortfall (!) due to the bank's disaster in south-eastern Europe and the related political mismanagement.

Political Economy of Privatization in Rich Democracies

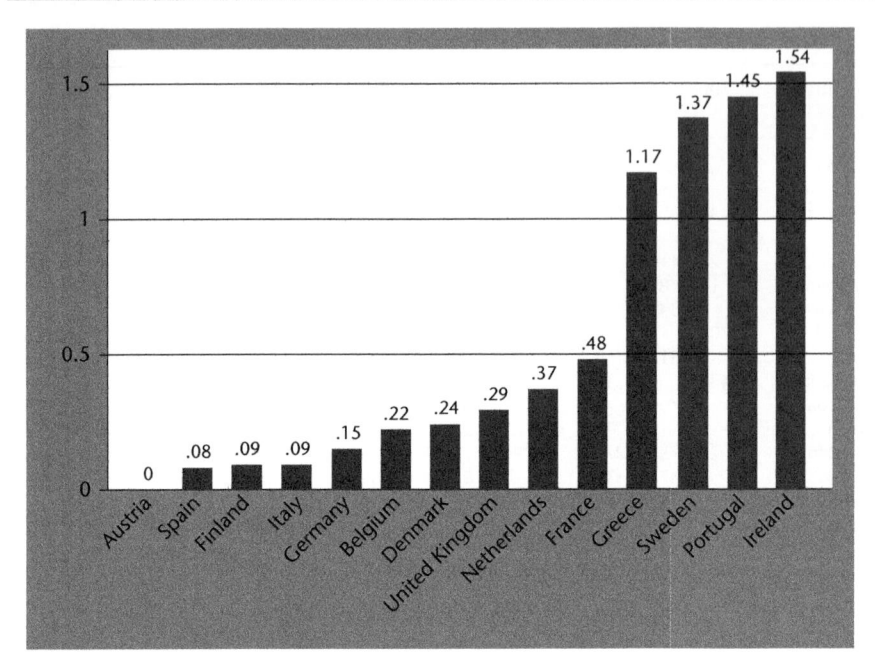

Figure 6.2. Cumulated privatization revenues of fourteen EU member countries as a percentage of GDP, 2008–13
Source: Privatization Barometer (<http://www.privatizationbarometer.net>) and OECD (<http://stats.oecd.org>)

Values by country: Austria 0, Spain .08, Finland .09, Italy .09, Germany .15, Belgium .22, Denmark .24, United Kingdom .29, Netherlands .37, France .48, Greece 1.17, Sweden 1.37, Portugal 1.45, Ireland 1.54.

privatization volume amounted to 1,067 billion US dollars. Revenues peaked in 2009 with 265.2 billion US dollars and the U.S. government turned out to be the world's largest privatizer as banks repurchased government holdings of preferred stocks equivalent to 168.8 billion US dollars.

Epilogue

How long-lasting is the recent recurrence of state intervention in the business sector? Did the economic crisis lead to a new balance between the state and the market or even to the end of the neo-liberal[2] *Zeitgeist*? While answering these questions involves a great deal of speculation, we nevertheless argue that the recent nationalization wave was only a temporary phenomenon. The bailouts of banks and insurance companies during the Great Recession have little in common with previous nationalizations in the industry sector or in the

---

[2] Note that the rise of the regulatory state is quite in contraction with neo-liberal postulations of deregulation (cf. Vogel 1998; Levi-Faur 2005).

utility sectors. It was neither intended by policy makers to put the wheel of history into reverse nor to fundamentally question the privatization and liberalization policies of the 1980s and 1990s. Quite on the contrary, state intervention and bail-outs served the main purpose of sustaining the market economy after the financial crisis at almost any price. Moreover, privatization quickly returned to the political agenda since governments were eager to reprivatize nationalized companies in order to recover the money spent on bail-outs. In our view, therefore, conclusions that '[t]he long movement toward market liberalization has stopped, and a new period of state intervention, reregulation, and creeping protectionism has begun' (Altman 2009: 2) or predictions of 'the end of neo-liberalism' are premature (cf. Comaroff 2011).

We rather assume that privatization will continue to play a major role in the near future since the global credit crunch ended up in a severe fiscal crisis. The dramatic increase in public debt since 2007 (see Table 6.3) will give rise to a long-lasting period of austerity in the majority of the long-term member states of the OECD. Confronted with exploding public debt, governments not only face enormous difficulties in raising the money required for any intended nationalizations, but they are also—irrespective of their partisan composition—forced to curb public expenditure and/or raise fresh revenues for the public purse. While spending cuts and tax increases are politically

Table 6.3. General government gross financial liabilities as a percentage of nominal GDP, 2007 vs. 2014

Country	2007	2014	Change
Australia	12.3	36.2	+23.9
Austria	77.6	103.4	+25.8
Belgium	93.6	119.2	+25.6
Canada	70.4	93.9	+23.5
Denmark	34.6	58.9	+24.3
Finland	40.1	68.4	+28.3
France	75.6	114.1	+38.5
Germany	63.9	79.0	+15.1
Greece	114.3	182.3	+68.0
Ireland	27.5	116.6	+89.1
Italy	111.8	146.9	+35.1
Japan	162.4	230.0	+67.6
Netherlands	48.5	77.8	+29.3
New Zealand	25.4	41.1	+16.0
Norway	56.6	35.1	−21.5
Portugal	78.1	142.4	+64.3
Spain	46.9	130.8	+83.9
Sweden	45.8	46.5	+0.7
Switzerland	49.9	42.6	−7.3
United Kingdom	45.3	95.9	+50.6
United States	64.3	109.7	+45.4

Source: OECD Economic Outlook 2014–2: 248

risky as well as controversial in democratic settings, privatizations once more might represent the lowest common denominator for reining in public debt. Our empirical analysis has shown that fiscal problem pressure has been a key trigger of privatization in the recent decades. We, therefore, expect that mounting fiscal problems and the concomitant harsh austerity policies will keep privatization on the political agenda in the years to come.

APPENDIX

Table A.1. The determinants of privatization: empirical test results

Reference	Operationalization of privatization determinant	Privatization indicator	Sample	Period	Design	Test result
Economic performance: GDP growth rates						
Boix (1997)	Average annual change of per capita GDP 1961–79, real values	Strategies towards public business sector (five categories from 5 = large privatizations to 1 = nationalizations)	OECD	1979–92	Ordered probit, cross-section of governments	Significant, probability of privatization decreases by almost 20 per cent per 1 per cent of GDP growth
		Privatization revenues over average annual GDP under each government	See above		OLS, cross-section of governments	Significant negative correlation, 1 per cent less growth increases revenues by 1.8 per cent of GDP
	Average annual growth rate, five years previous to year of government formation	See above				Insignificant
	Difference to average OECD growth rate	See above				Insignificant
Bortolotti et al. (2001)	Average growth rate (1970–96)	Number of sales (as percentage of number of domestic listed firms)	49 countries, all regions and economic development stages	1977–96	OLS, cross-section (averages)	Significant, 1 per cent lower growth leads to 1–2 per cent more sales
		Privatization revenues per capita (USD)	See above			Significant, 1 per cent lower growth leads to USD 122–70 more p.c. revenues
		Weighted average of stakes sold	See above			Significant, 1 per cent lower growth leads to about 5 per cent more stocks sold
		Number of public offers (PO) over total sales	See above			Weak significance, 1 per cent more growth leads to 5 per cent more (!) POs, insignificant if controlled for size of public sector

(*continued*)

Table A.1. Continued

Reference	Operationalization of privatization determinant	Privatization indicator	Sample	Period	Design	Test result
Bortolotti et al. (2003)	GDP growth (current values)	Major privatization deal observed (binary)	34 countries, all regions and economic development stages, except for transition economies	1977–99	Probit, pooled, fixed and random effects estimators	Insignificant
		Privatization revenues over GDP	See above		OLS, panel, fixed effects and random effects estimators	Insignificant
		Weighted average of stakes sold	See above			Insignificant
Belke et al. (2007)	GDP growth, one-year lags	Yearly privatization revenues over average GDP (1990–2001)	22 OECD countries	1990–2001	OLS, panel, fixed effects, time dummies	Insignificant
Zohlnhöfer et al. (2008)	Deviation from mean OECD growth (1985–95)	Cumulative privatization revenues normalized by average GDP	19 (20) OECD countries	1990–2000	OLS, cross-section	Significant, 1 per cent below average growth increases revenues by 1 per cent of GDP
Schmitt (2011)	Annual GDP growth rate	Index of Public Entrepreneurship (level of public involvement in telecom sector)	18 OECD countries	1980–2007	Spatial OLS and ML, Panel, country and period fixed effects	Insignificant (in eight of ten models), otherwise negative
Roberts and Saeed (2012)	Annual GDP growth rate	Number of privatization deals	13 OECD countries	1988–2006	Negative binomial regression	Insignificant
		Privatization revenues (scaled by GDP)			Tobit, random effects	Significant, growth increases privatization revenue
Schmitt (2013)	Annual GDP growth rate	Material privatization dummy for public utilities (telecom, railways, postal sectors)	21 OECD countries	1980–2007	Probit with cubic spline function	Insignificant
Schuster et al. (2013)	Annual GDP growth rate	Revenue Index (weighted revenues of SOEs over GDP)	20 OECD countries	1980–2007	ECM, panel, fixed effects	Weak significance, 1 per cent more growth decreases Revenue Index by 0.03 per cent of GDP

Author (Year)	Dependent variable	Independent variable	Sample	Period	Method	Result
		Employment Index (weighted employment in SOEs over total employment)	See above	See above	See above	Insignificant
Schmitt (2014a)	Annual GDP growth rate	Index of Public Entrepreneurship (level of public involvement in telecom, railways, and postal sectors)	15 European countries	1980–2007	Spatial OLS and ML, panel, country and period fixed effects	Insignificant
Economic performance: public budget deficit						
Boix (1997)	Public budget balance at first year of government	Strategies towards public business sector (five categories from 5 = large privatizations to 1 = nationalizations)	OECD	1979–92	Ordered probit, cross-section of governments	Insignificant
		Privatization revenues over average annual GDP under each government	See above		OLS, cross-section of governments	Insignificant
Bortolotti et al. (2001)	Average public deficit in three years before first privatization (normalized by GDP)	Number of sales (as percentage of number of domestic listed firms)	49 countries, all regions and economic development stages	1977–96	OLS, cross-section (averages)	Weak significance, higher deficit leads to more sales (insignificant if controlled for size of public sector)
		Privatization revenues per capita (USD)	See above			Insignificant
		Weighted average of stakes sold	See above			Weak significance, higher deficit leads to more stocks sold
		Number of public offers (PO) over total sales	See above			Significant only if controlled for size of public sector, higher deficit leads to less POs
Brune et al. (2004)	Budget balance (percentage of GDP), average of 1980–84	Cumulative privatization revenues (1985–99) over 1985 GDP	96 countries	1985–99	OLS, cross-section, Tobit	Significant negative correlation, one percentage point higher deficit increases revenues by 0.3 per cent of GDP

(continued)

Table A.1. Continued

Reference	Operationalization of privatization determinant	Privatization indicator	Sample	Period	Design	Test result
	Budget balance (percentage of GDP), one-year lags	Annual privatization revenues	See above		Panel, pooled OLS, time and region dummies	Insignificant
Meseguer (2004)	Public budget deficit (normalized by GDP)	Probability of launching privatization programme	23 OECD countries	1980–97	Dynamic probit	Insignificant
Henisz et al. (2005)	Budget balance over GDP	Privatization dummies for telecom and electricity-generation sectors	71 countries	1977–99	Multivariate probit (simulated ML), pooled cross-sections with country clustered standard errors	Insignificant
Belke et al. (2007)	General government financial balances (positive = surplus/negative = deficit), one-year lags	Yearly privatization revenues over average GDP (1990–2001)	22 OECD countries	1990–2001	OLS, panel, fixed effects, time dummies	Significant, negative, one percentage point deficit increases revenues by 0.4–0.6 per cent of GDP
Zohlnhöfer et al. (2008)	Budget deficit exceeds 3 per cent (dummy)	Cumulative privatization revenues normalized by average GDP	14 EU member states	1990–2000	OLS, panel (1990-4, 1995–7, 1998–2000)	Significant, violation of Maastricht criterion increases revenues by 0.38 per cent to 0.5 per cent of GDP
			20 OECD countries	See above	OLS, cross-section	Significant, deficit increases revenues by 0.62 per cent to 0.81 per cent of GDP
Fink (2011)	Public deficit (percentage of GDP), one-year lags	Decision to privatize telecom sector	21 OECD countries	1978–2008	Panel, event history analysis (Cox & Weibull models)	Insignificant
Schmitt (2011)	Public deficit (normalized by GDP)	Index of Public Entrepreneurship (level of public involvement in telecom sector)	18 OECD countries	1980–2007	Spatial OLS and ML, panel, country and period fixed effects	Insignificant (in nine of ten models), otherwise negative

Roberts and Saeed (2012)	Budget balance (normalized by GDP)	Number of privatization deals	13 OECD countries	1988–2006	Negative binomial regression	Insignificant
		Privatization revenues (scaled by GDP)			Tobit, random effects	Insignificant
Schmitt (2013)	Public deficit (normalized by GDP)	Material privatization dummy for public utilities (telecom, railways, postal sectors)	21 OECD countries	1980–2007	Probit with cubic spline function	Significant, public deficit increases likelihood of privatization
Schuster et al. (2013)	Public deficit (normalized by GDP)	Revenue Index (weighted revenues of SOEs over GDP)	20 OECD countries	1980–2007	ECM, panel, fixed effects	Insignificant
		Employment Index (weighted employment in SOEs over total employment)	See above			Significant positive effect
Schmitt (2014a)	Public deficit (normalized by GDP)	Index of Public Entrepreneurship (level of public involvement in telecom, railways and postal sectors)	15 European countries	1980–2007	Spatial OLS and ML, panel, country and period fixed effects	Significant positive coefficient
Economic performance: public debt						
Bortolotti et al. (2003)	Public debt, one-year lags	Major privatization deal observed (binary)	34 countries, all regions and economic development stages, except for transition economies	1977–99	Probit, pooled, fixed and random effects estimators	Significant, high-debt countries are more likely to privatize
		Privatization revenues over GDP	See above		OLS, panel, fixed effects and random effects estimators	Insignificant
		Weighted average of stakes sold	See above			Insignificant
Bortolotti and Pinotti (2008)	Public debt (normalized by GDP)	Median privatization revenues reached (hazard rate)	21 OECD countries	1977–2002	Panel, event history analysis (Cox and Weibull models)	Insignificant (in twenty-five of twenty-six models)
Schneider and Häge (2008)	Public debt (max. percentage of GDP 1983–97)	Privatization of public infrastructures (per cent)	20 OECD countries	1983–2000	OLS, cross-section	Insignificant

(continued)

Table A.1. Continued

Reference	Operationalization of privatization determinant	Privatization indicator	Sample	Period	Design	Test result
Schuster et al. (2013)	Public debt (normalized by GDP)	Revenue Index (weighted revenues of SOEs over GDP)	20 OECD countries	1980–2007	ECM, panel, fixed effects	Significant negative effect
		Employment Index (weighted employment in SOEs over total employment)	See above			Significant negative effect
Economic performance: unemployment						
Belke et al. (2007)	Unemployment rate, one-year lags	Yearly privatization revenues over average GDP (1990–2001)	22 OECD countries	1990–2001	OLS, fixed effects, time dummies	Significant, positive, 1 per cent of unemployment increases revenues by 0.06–0.12 per cent of GDP
Economic performance: inflation						
Meseguer (2004)	Annual inflation rate	Probability of launching privatization programme	23 OECD countries	1980–97	Dynamic probit	Insignificant
Roberts and Saeed (2012)	Annual inflation rate	Number of privatization deals	13 OECD countries	1988–2006	Negative binomial regression	Insignificant
		Privatization revenues (scaled by GDP)			Tobit, random effects	Significant, inflation decreases privatization revenues
Economic performance: stage of economic development						
Bortolotti et al. (2001)	Average annual GNP (1977–96, log)	Number of sales (as percentage of number of domestic listed firms)	49 countries, all regions and economic development stages	1977–96	OLS, cross-section (averages)	Insignificant
		Number of public offers (PO) over total sales	See above			Insignificant

Study	Variable	Measure	Sample	Period	Method	Result
Bortolotti et al. (2003)	GDP per capita (current values)	Major privatization deal observed (binary)	34 countries, all regions and economic development stages, except for transition economies	1977–99	Probit, pooled, fixed and random effects estimators	Significant, high-GDP countries are more likely to privatize
		Privatization revenues over GDP	See above		OLS, panel, fixed effects and random effects estimators	Insignificant
		Weighted average of stakes sold	See above		OLS, cross-section	Insignificant
Brune et al. (2004)	GDP per capita (log), average of 1980–4	Cumulative privatization revenues (1985–99) over 1985 GDP	96 countries	1985–99		Insignificant (significant if cumulated number of transactions only)
	GDP per capita (log), one-year lags	Annual privatization revenues	See above		Pooled OLS, time and region dummies	Insignificant
Henisz et al. (2005)	GDP per capita	Privatization dummies for telecom and electricity-generation sectors	71 countries	1977–99	Multivariate probit (simulated ML), pooled cross-sections with country clustered standard errors	Insignificant
Bortolotti and Pinotti (2008)	GDP per capita	Median privatization revenues reached (hazard rate)	21 OECD countries	1977–2002	Panel, event history analysis (Cox and Weibull models)	Insignificant (in twenty-five of twenty-six models)
Schmitt (2011)	GDP per capita	Index of Public Entrepreneurship (level of public involvement in telecom sector)	18 OECD countries	1980–2007	Spatial OLS and ML, panel, country and period fixed effects	Insignificant
Schmitt (2013)	GDP per capita	Material privatization dummy for public utilities (telecom, railways, postal sectors)	21 OECD countries	1980–2007	Probit with cubic spline function	Significant, negative impact in most regressions
Schuster et al. (2013)	GDP per capita (lagged)	Revenue Index (weighted revenues of SOEs over GDP)	20 OECD countries	1980–2007	ECM, panel, fixed effects	Insignificant
		Employment Index (weighted employment in SOEs over total employment)	See above			Insignificant

(continued)

Table A.1. Continued

Reference	Operationalization of privatization determinant	Privatization indicator	Sample	Period	Design	Test result
Schmitt (2014a)	GDP per capita	Index of Public Entrepreneurship (level of public involvement in telecom, railways, and postal sectors)	15 European countries	1980–2007	Spatial OLS and ML, panel, country and period fixed effects	Insignificant
Actor preferences: political partisanship						
Boix (1997)	Socialist control of government (proportion of cabinet portfolios held by socialist or communist parties)	Strategies towards public business sector (five categories from 5 = large privatizations to 1 = nationalizations)	OECD	1979–92	Ordered probit, cross-section of governments	Significant, probability of privatization decreases from 50 per cent with no socialist participation to 0 per cent with purely socialist government
		Privatization revenues over average annual GDP under each government	See above			Significant, under purely socialist government revenues decrease by 2.7 per cent of GDP as compared to non-socialist government
	Ideology Index (weighted position of parties in government on policy space)	Strategies towards public business sector (five categories from 5 = large privatizations to 1 = nationalizations)	See above			Significant, probability of privatization increases with anti-public ownership score
		Privatization revenues over average annual GDP under each government	See above			Significant, privatization revenues increase with anti-public ownership score
Bortolotti et al. (2001)	'Right' dummy (takes value 1 if majority of privatizations by democratic conservative government)	Number of sales (as percentage of number of domestic listed firms)	49 countries, all regions and economic development stages	1977–96	OLS, cross-section (averages)	Significant, conservative governments privatize about 6–7 per cent more firms
		Privatization revenues per capita (USD)	See above			Insignificant
		Weighted average of stakes sold	See above			Insignificant

Author	Variable	Dependent variable	Sample	Period	Method	Result
Bortolotti et al. (2003)		Number of public offers (PO) over total sales	See above			Significant, conservative governments prefer POs over direct sales
	'Right' dummy (takes value 1 if majority of privatizations by democratic conservative government)	Major privatization deal observed (binary)	34 countries, all regions and economic development stages, except for transition economies	1977–99	Probit, pooled, fixed and random effects estimators	Significant, conservative governments are more likely to privatize
		Privatization revenues over GDP	See above		OLS, panel, fixed effects and random effects estimators	Insignificant
		Weighted average of stakes sold	See above			Insignificant
	Election dummy (1 = year of an election, 0 otherwise)	Major privatization deal observed (binary)	34 countries, all regions and economic development stages, except for transition economies	1977–99	Probit, pooled, fixed and random effects estimators	Insignificant
		Privatization revenues over GDP	See above		OLS, panel, fixed effects and random effects estimators	Insignificant
		Weighted average of stakes sold	See above			Significant, in election years about 6 per cent of stakes is sold less than in non-election years
Meseguer (2004)	Ideology Index (left = 3, centre = 2, right = 1)	Probability of launching privatization programme	23 OECD countries	1980–97	Dynamic probit	Significant, left-wing governments privatize more
Schneider et al. (2005)	Cabinet seat share of conservative governments	Percentage of state ownership in three infrastructure service sectors	26 OECD countries	1970–2000	OLS, pooled time series	Insignificant (significant, positive, in cross-sections for 1980s)

(continued)

Table A.1. Continued

Reference	Operationalization of privatization determinant	Privatization indicator	Sample	Period	Design	Test result
Belke et al. (2007)	Share of right-party cabinet portfolios	Yearly privatization revenues over average GDP (1990–2001)	22 OECD countries	1990–2001	OLS, panel, fixed effects, time dummies	Significant, under purely conservative government privatization proceeds increase by 0.4–0.5 per cent of GDP
Zohlnhöfer et al. (2008)	Cabinet share of bourgeois parties	Cumulative privatization revenues normalized by average GDP	14 EU member states	1990–2000	OLS, panel (1990-4, 1995-7, 1998–2000)	Insignificant (significant for 1998–2000 cross-section)
			20 OECD countries	See above	OLS, cross-section	Significant, positive, bourgeois government privatizes about 10 per cent of GDP more than leftist government
Bortolotti and Pinotti (2008)	Partisan Index of government (1 = extreme left, 10 = extreme right)	Median privatization revenues reached (hazard rate)	21 OECD countries	1977–2002	Panel, event history analysis (Cox and Weibull models)	Significant, right orientation speeds up privatization activities
Schneider and Häge (2008)	Cabinet seat share of left-wing parties	Privatization of public infrastructures (per cent)	20 OECD countries	1983–2000	OLS, cross-section	Significant, negative
Fink (2011)	Cabinet seat share of left-wing parties	Decision to privatize telecom sector	21 OECD countries	1978–2008	Panel, event history analysis (Cox and Weibull models)	Insignificant
Schmitt (2011)	Cabinet seat share of left-wing parties	Index of Public Entrepreneurship (level of public involvement in telecom sector)	18 OECD countries	1980–2007	Spatial OLS and ML, panel, country and period fixed effects	Insignificant
Schmitt and Obinger (2011)	Cabinet seat share of left-wing parties	Privatization intensity	21 OECD countries	1980–2009	OLS, cross-section	Insignificant
Roberts and Saeed (2012)	Right-wing (1 if conservative party in office)	Number of privatization deals	13 OECD countries	1988–2006	Negative binomial regression	Insignificant

Author	Variable	Sample	Period	Method	Result
	Years in office	13 OECD countries		Tobit, random effects	Insignificant
	Number of privatization deals		1988–2006	Negative binomial regression	Insignificant
	Privatization revenues (scaled by GDP)			Tobit, random effects	Insignificant
Schmitt (2013)	Leftist government (cabinet seat share of left-wing parties)	21 OECD countries	1980–2007	Probit with cubic spline function	Significant, negative impact
Schuster et al. (2013)	Government ideology (index 0 = left, 10 = right)	20 OECD countries	1980–2007	ECM, panel, fixed effects	Significant, negative, right-wing governments speed up privatization in terms of revenues
	Employment Index (weighted employment in SOEs over total employment)	See above			Insignificant
Schmitt (2014a)	Index of Public Entrepreneurship (level of public involvement in telecom, railways, and postal sectors)	15 European countries	1980–2007	Spatial OLS and ML, panel, country and period fixed effects	Insignificant
Actor preferences: interest groups					
Belke et al. (2007)	Strike Activity Index (CPDS, Armingeon et al. 2008)	22 OECD countries	1990–2001	OLS, panel, fixed effects, time dummies	Significant, increasing strike activity leads to less privatization in terms of revenues over GDP
Bortolotti and Pinotti (2008)	Strike Activity Index (CPDS, Armingeon et al. 2008)	21 OECD countries	1977–2002	Panel, event history analysis (Cox and Weibull models)	Insignificant in most models
Zohlnhöfer et al. (2008)	Strike Activity Index (CPDS, Armingeon et al. 2008)	14 EU member states	1990–2000	OLS, panel (1990–4, 1995–7, 1998–2000)	Significant negative coefficient
		20 OECD countries	1990–2000	OLS, cross-section	Significant negative coefficient

(*continued*)

Table A.1. Continued

Reference	Operationalization of privatization determinant	Privatization indicator	Sample	Period	Design	Test result
Schmitt and Obinger (2011)	Labour union density (OECD)	Privatization intensity	21 OECD countries	1980–2009	OLS, cross-section	Insignificant
Schuster et al. (2013)	Strike Activity Index (CPDS, Armingeon et al. 2008)	Revenue Index (weighted revenues of SOEs over GDP)	20 OECD countries	1980–2007	ECM, panel, fixed effects	Insignificant
		Employment Index (weighted employment in SOEs over total employment)	See above			Insignificant
Institutions: consensus vs. majoritarian democracy						
Boix (1997)	Government Fragmentation Index (Rae 1968)	Strategies towards public business sector (five categories from 5 = large privatizations to 1 = nationalizations)	OECD	1979–92	Ordered probit, cross-section of governments	Significant, unified government increases privatization probability by forty-five percentage points as compared to most fragmented government
		Privatization revenues over average annual GDP under each government	See above		OLS, cross-section of governments	Significant, revenues increase by up to 5.4 per cent of GDP under unified government
	Majority government dummy (1 = yes, 0 = no)	Strategies towards public business sector (five categories from 5 = large privatizations to 1 = nationalizations)	See above		Ordered probit, cross-section of governments	Significant, privatization more likely under majoritarian government
		Privatization revenues over average annual GDP under each government	See above		OLS, cross-section of governments	Significant, privatization revenues up to 2.9 per cent of GDP higher under majoritarian government
Bortolotti and Pinotti (2008)	Effective number of parties (Laakso and Taagepera 1979), only government parties' seats	Median privatization revenues reached (hazard rate)	21 OECD countries	1977–2002	Panel, event history analysis (Cox and Weibull models)	Significant and negative in most models

		Effective number of parties (Laakso and Taagepera 1979), all parties	See above		Significant and negative in most models
		Disproportionality of electoral system (Gallagher 1991)	See above		Significant and positive in most models
Zohlnhöfer et al. (2008)		Cumulative privatization revenues normalized by average GDP	14 EU member states	1990–2000	OLS, panel (1990–4, 1995–7, 1998–2000)	Significant, minority government increases revenues by 1.4 per cent of GDP
	Minority government (percentage of time in office)				
	Fragmentation Index of government		20 OECD countries	1990–2000	OLS, cross-section	Insignificant
Institutions: veto players						
Henisz et al. (2005)	Political Constraints Index (POLCON) (Henisz 2000)	Privatization dummies for telecom and electricity-generation sectors	71 countries	1977–99	Multivariate probit (simulated ML), pooled cross-sections with country clustered standard errors	Insignificant
Schneider et al. (2005)	Veto Player Index (VPS) (Tsebelis 2002)	Percentage of state ownership in three infrastructure service sectors	26 OECD countries	1970–2000	OLS, pooled time series	Significant only for electricity sector, more veto players are associated with more state ownership
	Political Constraints Index (POLCON) (Henisz 2000)		See above			Insignificant
Belke et al. (2007)	Level of federalism (1 = centralized, 5 = decentralized)	Yearly privatization revenues over average GDP (1990–2001)	22 OECD countries	1990–2001	OLS, panel, fixed effects, time dummies	Insignificant
	Index of Institutional Veto Players (Keefer 2002)	Yearly privatization revenues over average GDP (1990–2001)	See above			Insignificant

(continued)

Table A.1. Continued

Reference	Operationalization of privatization determinant	Privatization indicator	Sample	Period	Design	Test result
Bortolotti and Pinotti (2008)	Federalism (dummy, 1 = federal structure, 0 = otherwise)	Median privatization revenues reached (hazard rate)	21 OECD countries	1977–2002	Panel, event history analysis (Cox and Weibull models)	Significant and positive in most models
Schneider and Häge (2008)	Index of Institutional Constraints (Schmidt 1996)	Privatization of public infrastructures (per cent)	20 OECD countries	1983–2000	OLS, cross-section	Insignificant
	Corporatism Index (Siaroff 1999)	Privatization of public infrastructures (per cent)	20 OECD countries	1983–2000	OLS, cross-section	Insignificant
Zohlnhöfer et al. (2008)	Index of Bicameralism, Federalism, and Constitutional Rigidity (Lijphart 1999)	Cumulative privatization revenues normalized by average GDP	14 EU member states	1990–2000	OLS, panel (1990–4, 1995–7, 1998–2000)	Significant negative coefficient
			20 OECD countries	1990–2000	OLS, cross-section	Significant negative coefficient
Fink (2011)	Political Constraints Index (POLCON) (Henisz 2000)	Decision to privatize telecom sector	21 OECD countries	1978–2008	Panel, event history analysis (Cox and Weibull models)	Insignificant
Schmitt (2011)	Index of Constitutional Structures (Huber et al. 1993, Armingeon et al. 2008)	Index of Public Entrepreneurship (level of public involvement in telecom sector)	18 OECD countries	1980–2007	Spatial OLS and ML, panel, country, and period fixed effects	Insignificant
Schmitt and Obinger (2011)	Corporatism Index (Siaroff 1999)	Privatization intensity	21 OECD countries	1980–2009	OLS, cross-section	Insignificant
Institutions: legal origin						
Bortolotti et al. (2001)	French law (dummy)	Weighted average of stakes sold	49 countries, all regions and economic development stages	1977–96	OLS, cross-section (averages)	Insignificant

						Significant, French civil law countries privatize twenty-five percentage points less stakes by public offers
	German law (dummy)	Weighted average of stakes sold	See above			Significant, German civil law countries privatize sixteen percentage points smaller stakes
		Number of public offers over total sales	See above			Insignificant
Bortolotti et al. (2003)	Dummies for common, French, German, and Scandinavian law	Major privatization deal observed (binary)	34 countries, all regions and economic development stages, except for transition economies	1977–99	Probit, pooled, fixed and random effects estimators	German law countries have significantly lower privatization probability
		Privatization revenues over GDP	See above		OLS, panel, fixed effects, and random effects estimators	Insignificant
		Weighted average of stakes sold	See above			French and German law countries sell 13 to 15 per cent less stakes
Brune et al. (2004)	Dummies for common, French and socialist law	Annual privatization revenues	96 countries	1985–99	Panel, pooled OLS, time, and region dummies	Significant and positive for all dummies
Institutions: capital market development						
Bortolotti et al. (2001)	Trade volume on the major stock exchange over GDP (Beck et al., 2000)	Privatization revenues per capita (USD)	49 countries, all regions and economic development stages	1977–96	IV (average savings, etc.), cross-section (averages)	Significant, 1 per cent more stock market volume in terms of GDP increases per capita revenues by 1,500 USD
		Weighted average of stakes sold	See above			Significant, 1 per cent more stock market volume in terms of GDP stakes sold by 0.63 percentage points

(continued)

Table A.1. Continued

Reference	Operationalization of privatization determinant	Privatization indicator	Sample	Period	Design	Test result
Bortolotti et al. (2003)	Indicators for stock market capitalization and liquidity, lagged by one year (Beck et al., 2000)	Major privatization deal observed (binary)	34 countries, all regions and economic development stages, except for transition economies	1977–99	Probit, pooled, fixed and random effects estimators	Both indicators significant, capitalization and liquidity make privatization more likely (endogeneity issues)
		Privatization revenues over GDP	See above		OLS, panel, fixed effects and random effects estimators	Insignificant
Brune et al. (2004)	Functioning stock market dummy (authors' own compilation)	Weighted average of stakes sold Cumulative privatization revenues (1985–99) over 1985 GDP	See above 96 countries	1985–99	OLS, cross-section, Tobit	Insignificant Significant, positive
		Annual privatization revenues	See above		Panel, pooled OLS, time and region dummies	Significant, positive (increases likelihood of privatization and revenues)
Bortolotti and Pinotti (2008)	Indicators for stock market capitalization and liquidity, lagged by one year (Beck et al., 2000)	Median privatization revenues reached (hazard rate)	21 OECD countries	1977–2002	Panel, event history analysis (Cox and Weibull models)	Insignificant in most models
Roberts and Saeed (2012)	Financial development (stocks traded as percentage of GDP)	Number of privatization deals	13 OECD countries	1988–2006	Negative binomial regression	Insignificant
		Privatization revenues (scaled by GDP)			Tobit, random effects	Insignificant
Schuster et al. (2013)	Capital market development (MSCI Country Index)	Revenue Index (weighted revenues of SOEs over GDP)	20 OECD countries	1980–2007	ECM, panel, fixed effects	Insignificant
		Employment Index (weighted employment in SOEs over total employment)	See above			Significant, better developed capital markets lead to more privatization

Author	Variable	Description	Sample	Period	Method	Result
Institutions: constitutional provisions						
Schmitt and Obinger (2011)	Index of Constitutional Barriers	Privatization intensity	21 OECD countries	1980–2009	OLS, cross-section	Significant negative influence of constitutional provisions on telecom and railways sector privatization, insignificant for postal sector
Schmitt (2013)	Index of constitutional protection (based on Schmitt and Obinger 2011)	Material privatization dummy for public utilities (telecom, railways, postal sectors)	21 OECD countries	1980–2007	Probit with cubic spline function	Insignificant
Schmitt (2014a)	Constitutional Index (Schmitt 2013, based on Schmitt and Obinger 2011)	Index of public entrepreneurship (level of public involvement in telecom, railways, and postal sectors)	15 European countries	1980–2007	Spatial OLS and ML, panel, country and period fixed effects	Significant, higher constitutional barriers lead to higher public involvement
Institutions: Initial size of the SOE sector						
Bortolotti et al. (2001)	Index of state ownership before first privatization (World Bank, 1995)	Number of sales (as percentage of number of domestic listed firms)	49 countries, all regions and economic development stages	1977–96	OLS, cross-section (averages)	Insignificant
		Privatization revenues per capita (USD)	See above			Insignificant
		Number of public offers (PO) over total sales	See above			Insignificant
Brune et al. (2004)	Size of SOE sector in 1980 (Gwartney et al. 1996)	Cumulative privatization revenues (1985–99) over 1985 GDP	96 countries	1985–99	OLS, cross-section, Tobit	Significant (positive) in baseline model, insignificant for developing countries
		Annual privatization revenues	See above		Panel, pooled OLS, time and region dummies	Significant (positive) in baseline model

(continued)

Table A.1. Continued

Reference	Operationalization of privatization determinant	Privatization indicator	Sample	Period	Design	Test result
Belke et al. (2007)	Economic Freedom Index, current values (Gwartney and Lawson 2004)	Yearly privatization revenues over average GDP (1990–2001)	22 OECD countries	1990–2001	OLS, panel, fixed effects, time dummies	Significant, more freedom leads to more privatization (endogeneity?)
Bortolotti and Pinotti (2008)	OECD index of public ownership in 1977 (Conway and Nicoletti, 2006)	Median privatization revenues reached (hazard rate)	21 OECD countries	1977–2002	Panel, Event history analysis (Cox & Weibull models)	Insignificant (in most models)
Zohlnhöfer et al. (2008)	CEEP Index of Public Ownership	Cumulative privatization revenues normalized by average GDP	14 EU member states	1990–2000	OLS, panel (1990–4,1995–7, 1998–2000)	Significant, positive, higher initial size associated with higher proceeds
	Size of SOE sector in 1990 (Gwartney and Lawson 2000)		20 OECD countries	1990–2000	OLS, cross-section	Significant, positive, higher initial size associated with higher proceeds
	Economic Freedom Index in 1990 (Gwartney and Lawson 2000)		See above			Significant, negative, more economic freedom associated with higher proceeds
Roberts and Saeed (2012)	Economic Freedom Index	Number of privatization deals	13 OECD countries	1988–2006	Negative binomial regression	Insignificant
		Privatization revenues (scaled by GDP)			Tobit, random effects	Insignificant; significant interactions with GDP growth (negative) and inflation (positive)
International influences: economic integration						
Brune et al. (2004)	Trade openness (exports plus imports over GDP)	Annual privatization revenues	96 countries	1985–99	Panel, pooled OLS, time and region dummies	Insignificant

Meseguer (2004)	Trade openness (exports plus imports over GDP)	Probability of launching privatization programme	23 OECD countries	1980–97	Dynamic probit	Insignificant
Schneider et al. (2005)	Financial openness (Quinn 1997)	Percentage of state ownership in three infrastructure service sectors	26 OECD countries	1970–2000	OLS, pooled time series	Significant, openness to capital flows decreases state ownership
	Trade openness (exports plus imports over GDP)	See above				Insignificant
	Inward FDI	See above				Insignificant
Belke et al. (2007)	Trade openness (exports plus imports over GDP)	Yearly privatization revenues over average GDP (1990–2001)	22 OECD countries	1990–2001	OLS, panel, fixed effects, time dummies	Significant, positive, 1 per cent trade openness increases revenues by 0.03 per cent of GDP
Zohlnhöfer et al. (2008)	Inward FDI stock over GDP	Cumulative privatization revenues normalized by average GDP	14 EU member states	1990–2000	OLS, panel (1990–4, 1995–7, 1998–2000)	Insignificant
	Financial openness (Quinn, 1997)		20 OECD countries	See above	OLS, cross-section	Insignificant
Schneider and Häge (2008)	Trade openness (exports plus imports over GDP)	Privatization of public infrastructures (per cent)	20 OECD countries	1983–2000	OLS, cross-section	Insignificant
	Index of capital mobility	See above				Insignificant
Fink (2011)	Financial openness (Quinn 1997)	Decision to privatize telecom sector	21 OECD countries	1978–2008	Panel, event history analysis (Cox and Weibull models)	Insignificant
Schmitt (2011)	Trade openness (exports plus imports over GDP)	Index of public entrepreneurship (level of public involvement in telecom sector)	18 OECD countries	1980–2007	Spatial OLS and ML, panel, country and period fixed effects	Insignificant
Schuster et al. (2013)	Trade openness (exports plus imports over GDP)	Revenue Index (weighted revenues of SOEs over GDP)	20 OECD countries	1980–2007	ECM, panel, fixed effects	Insignificant
		Employment Index (weighted employment in SOEs over total employment)	See above			Insignificant

(continued)

Table A.1. Continued

Reference	Operationalization of privatization determinant	Privatization indicator	Sample	Period	Design	Test result
Schmitt (2013)	Trade openness (exports plus imports over GDP)	Material privatization dummy for public utilities (telecom, railways, postal sectors)	21 OECD countries	1980–2007	Probit with cubic spline function	Insignificant
Schmitt (2014a)	Trade openness (exports plus imports over GDP)	Index of public entrepreneurship (level of public involvement in telecom, railways, and postal sectors)	15 European countries	1980–2007	Spatial OLS and ML, panel, country and period fixed effects	Insignificant

International influences: Europeanization

Reference	Operationalization of privatization determinant	Privatization indicator	Sample	Period	Design	Test result
Meseguer (2004)	EU membership (dummy)	Probability of launching privatization programme	23 OECD countries	1980–97	Dynamic probit	Insignificant
Schneider and Häge (2008)	EU membership (dummy)	Privatization of public infrastructures (per cent)	20 OECD countries	1983–2000	OLS, cross-section	Significant, EU membership increases infrastructure privatization by 18–31 percentage points
Fink (2011)	EU membership (dummy)	Decision to privatize telecom sector	21 OECD countries	1978–2008	Panel, event history analysis (Cox and Weibull models)	Significant, EU membership increases likelihood of privatization
Schmitt (2011)	EU membership (dummy)	Index of public entrepreneurship (level of public involvement in telecom sector)	18 OECD countries	1980–2007	Spatial OLS and ML, panel, country and period fixed effects	Insignificant
Schmitt and Obinger (2011)	EU membership (dummy)	Privatization intensity	21 OECD countries	1980–2009	OLS, cross-section	Significant in telecom and insignificant in postal sectors, weak negative impact in railways sector
Schmitt (2013)	EU membership (dummy)	Material privatization dummy for public utilities (telecom, railways, postal sectors)	21 OECD countries	1980–2007	Probit with cubic spline function	Significant, positive for telecom and post, negative for railways
Schuster et al. (2013)	EU membership (dummy) and EU accession	Revenue Index (weighted revenues of SOEs over GDP)	20 OECD countries	1980–2007	ECM, panel, fixed effects	Insignificant

Study	Variable	Sample	Period	Method	Result
	Employment Index (weighted employment in SOEs over total employment)	See above			Insignificant
Schmitt (2014a)	EU membership				
	Index of Public Entrepreneurship (level of public involvement in telecom, railways, and postal sectors)	15 European countries	1980–2007	Spatial OLS and ML, panel, country and period fixed effects	Significant and negative in 2/4 regressions
International influences: policy diffusion					
Meseguer (2004)	Privatization experience (growth rates of privatization countries as compared to non-privatization countries)	Probability of launching privatization programme	23 OECD countries	1980–97	Dynamic probit	Significant, positive impact
	Herding (number of countries with privatization activities)	Probability of launching privatization programme	23 OECD countries	1980–97	Dynamic probit	Significant, positive impact
Fink (2011)	Cross-country diffusion	Decision to privatize telecom sector	21 OECD countries	1978–2008	Panel, event history analysis (Cox and Weibull models)	Significant, positive impact
	Cross-sector diffusion		See above			Insignificant
Schmitt (2011)	Spatial lags (several different specifications)	Index of Public Entrepreneurship (level of public involvement in telecom sector)	18 OECD countries	1980–2007	Spatial OLS and ML, panel, country and period fixed effects	Distance and trade lags significant
Schmitt (2014a)	Cross-sector diffusion	Index of public entrepreneurship (level of public involvement in telecom, railways, and postal sectors)	15 European countries	1980–2007	Spatial OLS and ML, panel, country and period fixed effects	Insignificant
	Spatial lags (several different specifications)		See above			Trade relations and interaction with trade openness significant

The following table summarizes the operationalization of the central variables.

Table A.2. Operationalization and data sources

Variable	Description	Source
a) Variables used in Chapter 5		
Public Entrepreneurship$_{t-1}$	Lagged values of public entrepreneurship	Own data source
GDP per capita (log.)	Logged values of real GDP per capita	Heston et al. 2012 (PWT 7.1)
GDP growth	Compound annual growth rate of real GDP per capita	Heston et al. 2012 (PWT 7.1)
Public debt	Gross government debt (financial liabilities as a percentage of GDP	Armingeon et al. (2011) Comparative political data set
Trade openness	Sum of imports and exports as a percentage of GDP in constant prices (2005)	Heston et al. 2012 (PWT 7.1)
Left-leaning cabinet	Cabinet seats of social democratic and communist parties as a percentage of total cabinet posts	Data kindly provided by Manfred G. Schmidt, University of Heidelberg
Union density	Net union membership as a proportion of wage and salary earners in employment	Armingeon et al. (2011), comparative political data set
Political institutions	PolconIII: index of political constraints that estimates the feasibility of policy change (for details see Henisz 2002	Henisz 2010
b) Variables only used in Chapter 5, section 2		
Constitutional barriers	Additive index described in detail in section 2	Own data source
EU membership	Length of the EU membership of a country as a percentage of the observation period	Own calculation
Δ Trade openness	Trade openness, average 1980–2007	Heston et al. 2012 (PWT 7.1)
Δ Union density	Union density, difference between 1980 and 2007	Armingeon et al. (2011), comparative political data set
Ø Union density	Union density, average 1980–2007	Armingeon et al. (2011), comparative political data set
GDP growth	GDP growth, average 1980–2007	Heston et al. 2012 (PWT 7.1)
Left-wing cabinet	Cabinet seats of social democratic and communist parties as a percentage of total cabinet posts, average 1980–2006	Data kindly provided by Manfred G. Schmidt, University of Heidelberg

c) Variables only used in Chapter 5, section 3

Conservative cabinet	Cabinet seats of secular conservative parties as a percentage of total cabinet posts	Data kindly provided by Manfred G. Schmidt, University of Heidelberg Döring and Manow 2011
Ideological position	Ideological position of the government on a left–right scale. The ideological position of each party in government is weighted by the seats of that party in parliament in relation to the total number of parliament seats held by cabinet parties	Own assessment
Maastricht	Governments of EU member countries in power sometime between 1993 (ratification of the Maastricht Treaty) and 1997 (reference year for EMU participation) = 1 and 0 otherwise	Own assessment
Years in power	Cabinet duration in years	Own assessment
Initial size of public entrepreneurship	Index of Public Entrepreneurship in the starting year of the cabinet	Own data source

d) Variables only used in Chapter 5, section 4

Spatial lag (trade)	Weighting matrix is generated by using sum of exports and imports between two countries as a percentage of the total trade volume of a country. The weighting matrix is row-standardized	Direction of Trade Statistics (IMF)
Spatial lag (distance)	Weighting matrix is generated by using the inverse distance between capitals in km. The weighting matrix is row-standardized	Own calculation
Spatial lag (competition)	Weighting matrix is generated by using the correlation between the trade volume of each pair of countries to all other trade. The weighting matrix is row-standardized	Own calculation based on Direction of Trade Statistics (IMF)
Spatial lag (EU)	Weighting matrix is generated by using the EU membership. Cells equal 1 if two countries both belong to the European Union, otherwise 0. The weighting matrix is row-standardized	Own calculation

References

Alesina, A. (1987): 'Macroeconomic Policy in a Two-Party System as a Repeated Game', *Quarterly Journal of Economics* **102**, 3, 651–78.
Alesina, A. and A. Drazen (1991): 'Why Are Stabilizations Delayed?', *American Economic Review* **81**, 5, 1170–88.
Alesina, A. and H. Rosenthal (1995): *Partisan Politics, Divided Government, and the Economy*. Cambridge: Cambridge University Press.
Alesina, A. and H. Rosenthal (1996): 'A Theory of Divided Government', *Econometrica* **64**, 6, 1311–41.
Alesina, A., N. Roubini, and G. D. Cohen (1997): *Political Cycles and the Macroeconomy*. Cambridge, MA: MIT Press.
Altman, R. C. (2009): 'Globalization in Retreat: Further Geopolitical Consequences of the Financial Crisis', *Foreign Affairs* **88**, 4, 2–7.
Amatori, F. (2000): 'Beyond State and Market: Italy's Futile Search for a Third Way', in: P. M. Toninelli (ed.): *The Rise and Fall of State-Owned Enterprise in the Western World*, 128–56. Cambridge: Cambridge University Press.
Ambrosius, G. (2000): 'Services Publics, Leistungen der Daseinsvorsorge oder Universaldienste? Zur historischen Dimension eines zukünftigen Elements europäischer Gesellschaftspolitik', in: H. Cox (ed.): *Daseinsvorsorge und öffentliche Dienstleistungen in der Europäischen Union*. Baden-Baden: Nomos.
Anselin, L. (2003): 'Spatial Externalities, Spatial Multipliers, and Spatial Econometrics', *International Regional Science Review* **26**, 2, 153–66.
Anselin, L., A. Bera, R. J. Florax, and M. Yoon (1996): 'Simple Diagnostic Tests for Spatial Dependence', *Regional Science and Urban Economics* **26**, 1, 77–104.
Armingeon, K., P. Leimgruber, M. Beyeler, and S. Menegale (2008): *Comparative Political Data Set 1960–2006*. Bern: University of Bern.
Armingeon, K., P. Leimgruber, M. Beyeler, and S. Menegale (2011): *Comparative Political Data Set I 1960–2008*. Bern: Institute of Political Science, University of Berne.
Arocena, P. and D. Oliveros (2012): 'The Efficiency of State-Owned and Privatized Firms: Does Ownership Make a Difference?', *International Journal of Production Economics* **140**, 1, 457–65.
Auby, J.-F. and O. Raymundie (2003): *Le service public: droit national et droit communautaire, modes de gestion*. Paris: Éditions du Moniteur.
Barjot, D. (2011): 'Public Utilities and Private Initiative: The French Concession Model in Historical Perspective', *Business History* **53**, 5, 782–800.
Beck, T., A. Demirgüç-Kunt, and R. Levine (2000): 'A New Database on the Structure and Development of the Financial Sector', *World Bank Economic Review* **14**, 3, 597–605.

References

Beck, T., A. Demirgüç-Kunt, and R. Levine (2003): 'Law and Finance: Why Does Legal Origin Matter?', *Journal of Comparative Economics* 31, 4, 653–75.

Belke, A., F. Baumgärtner, F. Schneider, and R. Setzer (2007): 'The Different Extent of Privatization Proceeds in OECD Countries: A Preliminary Explanation Using a Public-Choice Approach', *Finanzarchiv* 63, 2, 211–43.

Bell, J. (2007): 'Administrative Law in a Comparative Perspective', in: E. Örücü and D. Nelken (eds.): *Comparative Law: A Handbook*, 287–312. Oxford: Hart Publishing.

Biais, B. and E. Perotti (2002): 'Machiavellian Privatization', *American Economic Review* 92, 1, 240–58.

Birdsall, N. and J. Nellis (2003): 'Winners and Losers: Assessing the Distributional Impact of Privatization', *World Development* 31, 10, 1617–33.

Bogart, D. (2009): 'Nationalizations and the Development of Transport Systems: Cross-Country Evidence from Railroad Networks, 1860–1912', *Journal of Economic History* 69, 1, 202–37.

Boix, C. (1997): 'Privatizing the Public Business Sector in the Eighties: Economic Performance, Partisan Responses and Divided Governments', *British Journal of Political Science* 27, 4, 473–96.

Bordo, M. D., B. Eichengreen, and D. A. Irwin (1999): *Is Globalization Today Really Different than Globalization a Hundred Years Ago?* NBER Working Paper No. W7195. Cambridge, MA: NBER.

Bortolotti, B. and P. Pinotti (2008): 'Delayed Privatization', *Public Choice* 136, 3–4, 331–51.

Bortolotti, B., M. Fantini, and D. Siniscalo (2001): 'Privatisation: Politics, Institutions, and Financial Markets', *Emerging Markets Review* 2, 2, 109–36.

Bortolotti, B., M. Fantini, and D. Siniscalo (2003): 'Privatisation around the World: Evidence from Panel Data', *Journal of Public Economics* 88, 1, 305–32.

Boston, J. (1987): 'Transforming New Zealand's Public Sector: Labour's Quest for Improved Efficiency and Accountability', *Public Administration* 65, 4, 423–42.

Boutchkova, M. K. and W. L. Megginson (2000): 'Privatization and the Rise of Global Capital Markets', *Financial Management* 29, 4, 31–75.

Boycko, M., A. Shleifer, and R. W. Vishny (1994): 'Voucher Privatization', *Journal of Financial Economics* 35, 2, 249–66.

Braconnier, S. (2003): *Droit des services publics*. Paris: Presses Universitaires.

Breen, M. and D. Doyle (2013): 'The Determinants of Privatization: A Comparative Analysis of Developing Countries', *Journal of Comparative Policy Analysis* 15, 1, 1–20.

Brown, D. J., J. S. Earle, and Á. Telegdy (2010): 'Employment and Wage Effects of Privatization: Evidence from Hungary, Romania, Russia and Ukraine', *Economic Journal* 120, 545, 683–708.

Brune, N., G. Garrett, and B. Kogut (2004): 'The International Monetary Fund and the Global Spread of Privatization', *IMF Staff Papers* 51, 2, 195–219.

Budge, I., H.-D. Klingemann, A. Volkens, J. Bara, and E. Tannenbaum (2001): *Mapping Policy Preferences: Estimates for Parties, Electors, and Governments 1945–1998*. Oxford: Oxford University Press.

Carlsson, B. (1988a): 'Public Industrial Enterprises in Norway: A Comparison with Sweden', *Annals of Public and Cooperative Economics* 59, 2, 197–213.

References

Carlsson, B. (1988b): 'Public Industrial Enterprises in Sweden: Searching for a Viable Structure', *Annals of Public and Cooperative Economics* **59**, 2, 175–95.

Carreras, A., X. Tafunell, and E. Torres (2000): 'The Rise and Decline of Spanish State-Owned Firms', in: P. M. Toninelli (ed.): *The Rise and Fall of State-Owned Enterprise in the Western World*, 208–36. Cambridge: Cambridge University Press.

Castles, F. G. (1998): *Comparative Public Policy: Patterns of Post-War Transformation*. Cheltenham: Edward Elgar.

Castles, F. G. (2006): *The Growth of the Post-War Public Expenditure State: Long-Term Trajectories and Recent Trends*. Transtate Working Paper No. 35. Bremen: University of Bremen.

Chadeau, E. (2000): 'The Rise and Decline of State-Owned Industry in Twentieth-Century France', in: P. M. Toninelli (ed.): *The Rise and Fall of State-Owned Enterprise in the Western World*, 185–207. Cambridge: Cambridge University Press.

Christodoulakis, N. and Y. Katsoulacos (1993): *Privatization, Public Deficit Finance, and Investment in Infrastructure*. Discussion Paper 831. London: Centre for Economic Policy Research.

Clifton, J., F. Comin, and D. Diaz Fuentes (2003): *Privatisation in the European Union: Public Enterprises and Integration*. Dordrecht: Kluwer.

Clifton, J., P. Lanthier, and H. Schröter (2011): 'Regulating and Deregulating the Public Utilities 1830–2010', *Business History* **53**, 5, 659–72.

Coch, L. and J. R. P. French, Jr. (1948): 'Overcoming Resistance to Change', *Human Relations* **1**, 512–32.

Comaroff, J. (2011): 'The End of Neoliberalism? What Is Left of the Left', *Annals of the American Academy of Political and Social Science* **637**, 1, 141–7.

Conway, P. and G. Nicoletti (2006): *Product Market Regulation in the Non-Manufacturing Sectors of OECD Countries: Measurement and Highlights*. OECD Economics Department Working Paper 530. Paris: OECD.

Davids, M. and J. L. van Zanden (2000): 'A Reluctant State and Its Enterprises: State-Owned Enterprises in the Netherlands in the 'Long' Twentieth Century', in: P. M. Toninelli (ed.): *The Rise and Fall of State-Owned Enterprise in the Western World*, 253–72. Cambridge: Cambridge University Press.

De Boef, S. and L. Keele (2008): 'Taking Time Seriously', *American Journal of Political Science* **52**, 1, 184–200.

De Swaan, A. (1988): *In Care of the State: Health Care, Education and Welfare in Europe and America*. Oxford: Oxford University Press.

Dobbin, F., B. Simmons, and G. Garrett (2007): 'The Global Diffusion of Public Policies: Social Construction, Coercion, Competition, or Learning?', *Annual Review of Sociology* **33**, 449–72.

Döring, H. and P. Manow (2011): *Parliament and Government Composition Database (ParlGov)*. Version 11/07–26 July. Bremen: University of Bremen.

Doyle, D. (2012): 'Pressures to Privatize? The IMF, Globalization, and Partisanship in Latin America', *Political Research Quarterly* **65**, 3, 572–85.

Dreyfus, M. (2009): 'France', in: M. Krajewski, U. Neergaard, and J. van de Gronden (eds): *The Changing Legal Framework for Services of General Interest in Europe: Between Competition and Solidarity*, 269–90. Den Haag: Asser.

References

Elkins, Z. and B. Simmons (2005): 'On Waves, Clusters, and Diffusion: A Conceptual Framework', *Annals of the American Academy of Political and Social Science* **598**, 1, 33–51.

Ennser-Jedenastik, L. (2013): 'Die parteipolitische Besetzung von Spitzenpositionen in österreichischen Staatsunternehmen', *Austrian Journal of Political Science* **42**, 2, 125–43.

Esping-Andersen, G. (1990): *The Three Worlds of Welfare Capitalism*. Princeton, NJ: Princeton University Press.

Estrin, S., J. Hanousek, E. Kocenda, and J. Svejnar (2009): 'The Effects of Privatization and Ownership in Transition Economies', *Journal of Economic Literature* **47**, 3, 699–728.

Evangelopoulos, P. (2012): 'Rent Seeking in the Greek Drama', *Independent Review* **17**, 1, 95–8.

Feigenbaum, H., J. Henig, and C. Hamnett (1998): *Shrinking the State: The Political Underpinnings of Privatization*. Cambridge: Cambridge University Press.

Fernandez, R. and D. Rodrik (1991): 'Resistance to Reform: Status Quo Bias in the Presence of Individual-Specific Uncertainty', *American Economic Review* **81**, 5, 1146–55.

Fink, S. (2011): 'A Contagious Concept: Explaining the Spread of Privatization in the Telecommunications Sector', *Governance* **24**, 1, 111–39.

Fiorina, M. P. (1996): *Divided Government*, 2nd edition. Boston, MA: Allyn and Bacon.

Fischer, S. (1977): 'Long-Term Contracts, Rational Expectations and the Optimal Money Supply Rule', *Journal of Political Economy* **85**, 1, 191–206.

Forsthoff, E. (1938): *Die Verwaltung als Leistungsträger*. Stuttgart: Kohlhammer.

Franzese, R. J., Jr. (2002): 'Electoral and Partisan Cycles in Economic Policies and Outcomes', *Annual Review of Political Science* **5**, 1, 369–421.

Franzese, R. J., Jr. and J. C. Hays (2007): 'Spatial Econometric Models of Cross-Sectional Interdependence in Political Science Panel and Time-Series-Cross-Section Data', *Political Analysis* **15**, 2, 140–64.

Franzese, R. J., Jr. and J. C. Hays (2008): 'Interdependence in Comparative Politics: Substance, Theory, Empirics, Substance', *Comparative Political Studies* **41**, 4–5, 742–80.

Frey, B. S. and F. Schneider (1978a): 'An Empirical Study of Politico-Economic Interaction in the United States', *Review of Economics and Statistics* **60**, 2, 174–83.

Frey, B. S. and F. Schneider (1978b): 'A Politico-Economic Model of the United Kingdom', *Economic Journal* **88**, 350, 243–53.

Friedman, M. (1968): 'The Role of Monetary Policy', *American Economic Review* **58**, 1, 1–17.

Galambos, L. (2000): 'State-Owned Enterprises in a Hostile Environment: The U.S. Experience', in: P. M. Toninelli (ed.): *The Rise and Fall of State-Owned Enterprise in the Western World*, 273–302. Cambridge: Cambridge University Press.

Gallagher, M. (1991): 'Proportionality, Disproportionality and Electoral Systems', *Electoral Studies* **10**, 1, 33–51.

Garret, G. (1998): *Partisan Politics in the Global Economy*. Cambridge: Cambridge University Press.

References

Gilardi, F. (2005): 'The Institutional Foundation of Regulatory Capitalism: The Diffusion of Independent Regulatory Agencies in Europe', *Annals of the American Academy of Political and Social Science* **598**, 84–101.

Gilardi, F. (2010): 'Who Learns from What in Policy Diffusion Processes?', *American Journal of Political Science* **54**, 3, 650–66.

Glasserman, P. and Z. Wang (2011): 'Valuing the Treasury's Capital Assistance Program', *Management Science* **57**, 7, 1195–211.

Glenn, P. (2007): *Legal Traditions of the World: Sustainable Diversity in Law*. Oxford: Oxford University Press.

Graham, C. (2000): *Regulating Public Utilities: A Constitutional Approach*. Oxford: Oxford University Press.

Graham, C. and T. Prosser (2003): *Privatizing Public Enterprises: Constitutions, the State, and Regulation in Comparative Perspective*. Oxford: Oxford University Press.

Grassini, F. A. (1981): 'The Italian Enterprises: The Political Constraints', in: R. Vernon and Y. Aharoni (eds): *State-Owned Enterprise in the Western Economies*, 70–84. London: Croom Helm.

Gwartney, J. and R. Lawson (2000): *Economic Freedom of the World: 2000 Annual Report*. Vancouver: Fraser Institute.

Gwartney, J. and R. Lawson (2004): *Economic Freedom of the World: 2004 Annual Report*. Vancouver: Fraser Institute.

Gwartney, J., R. Lawson, and W. Block (1996): *Economic Freedom of the World: 1975–1995*. Vancouver: Fraser Institute.

Hall, P. A. (1986): *Governing the Economy: The Politics of State Intervention in France and Britain*. Oxford: Oxford University Press.

Heckman, J. J. (1979): 'Sample Selection Bias as a Specification Error', *Econometrica* **47**, 1, 153–61.

Heichel, S., J. Pape, and T. Sommerer (2005): 'Is There Convergence in Convergence Research? An Overview of Empirical Studies on Policy Convergence', *Journal of European Public Policy* **12**, 5, 817–40.

Hellermann, J. (2001): 'Daseinsvorsorge im europäischen Vergleich', in: Schader-Stiftung (ed.): *Die Zukunft der Daseinsvorsorge: Öffentliche Unternehmen im Wettbewerb*, 78–100. Darmstadt: Schader-Stiftung.

Henisz, W. J. (2000): 'The Institutional Environment for Economic Growth', *Economics and Politics* **12**, 1, 1–31.

Henisz, W. J. (2002): *The Political Constraint Index (POLCON) Dataset*. Philadelphia: Wharton School, University of Pennsylvania.

Henisz, W. J. (2010): *The Political Constraint Index (POLCON) Dataset*. Philadelphia: Wharton School, University of Pennsylvania, Philadelphia.

Henisz, W. J., B. A. Zelner, and M. F. Guillén (2005): 'The Worldwide Diffusion of Market-Oriented Infrastructure Reform, 1977–1999', *American Sociological Review* **70**, 6, 871–97.

Heston, A., R. Summers, and B. Aten (2012): *Penn World Table Version 7.1*. Center for International Comparisons of Production, Income, and Prices at the University of Pennsylvania, Philadelphia.

References

Hibbs, D. A., Jr. (1975): *Economic Interest and the Politics of Macroeconomic Policy*. Cambridge, MA: Center for International Studies, MIT.

Hibbs, D. A., Jr. (1977): 'Political Parties and Macroeconomic Policy', *American Political Science Review* **71**, 4, 1467–87.

Hibbs, D. A., Jr. (1978): 'On the Political Economy of Long-Run Trends in Strike-Activity', *British Journal of Political Science* **8**, 2, 153–75.

Hibbs, D. A., Jr. (1986): 'Political Parties and Macroeconomic Policies and Outcomes in the United States', *American Economic Review* **76**, 2, 66–70.

Hibbs, D. A., Jr. (1992): 'Partisan Theory after Fifteen Years', *European Journal of Political Economy* **8**, 3, 361–73.

Hibbs, D. A., Jr. (2006): 'Voting and the Macroeconomy', in: B. R. Weingast and D. A. Wittman (eds): *The Oxford Handbook of Political Economy*, 565–86. Oxford: Oxford University Press.

Hodge, G. A., C. Greve, and A. E. Boardman (eds) (2010): *International Handbook on Public-Private Partnership*. Cheltenham: Edward Elgar.

Holmström, B. and J. Tirole (1993): 'Market Liquidity and Performance Monitoring', *Journal of Political Economy* **101**, 4, 678–709.

Holzinger, K. and C. Knill (2005): 'Causes and Conditions of Cross-National Policy Convergence', *Journal of European Public Policy* **12**, 5, 775–96.

Holzinger, K. and S. K. Schmidt (2015): 'From the Positive to the Regulatory State: A Transformation in the Machinery of Governance?', in: S. Leibfried, E. Huber, M. Lange, J. D. Levy, F. Nullmeier, and J. D. Stephens (eds): *The Oxford Handbook of Transformations of the State*, 499–515. Oxford: Oxford University Press.

Höpner, M., A. Petring, D. Seikel, and B. Werner (2011): 'Liberalisierungspolitik: Eine Bestandsaufnahme des Rückbaus sozial- und wirtschaftspolitischer Interventionen in entwickelten Industrieländern', *Kölner Zeitschrift für Soziologie und Sozialpsychologie* **63**, 1, 1–32.

Huber, E., C. Ragin, and J. D. Stephens (1993): 'Social Democracy, Christian Democracy, Constitutional Structure, and the Welfare State', *American Journal of Sociology* **99**, 3, 711–49.

IMF (2009): *World Economic Outlook*. Washington, DC: International Monetary Fund.

Jäger, A. (2004): 'Der Zusammenhang von Staat und Infrastruktur und die Privatisierung von Infrastrukturen aus staatstheoretischer Perspektive', in: V. Schneider and M. Tenbücken (eds): *Der Staat auf dem Rückzug*, 29–52. Frankfurt a. M.: Campus.

Jamasb, T. and M. Pollitt (2005): 'Electricity Market Reform in the European Union: Review of Progress toward Liberalization and Integration', *Energy Journal* **26**, Special Issue: European Electricity Liberalization, 11–41.

Jordana, J., D. Levi-Faur, and X. Fernandez i Marin (2011): 'The Global Diffusion of Regulatory Agencies: Channels of Transfer and Stages of Diffusion', *Comparative Political Studies* **44**, 10, 1343–69.

Keefer, P. (2002): 'Politics and the Determinants of Banking Crises: The Effects of Political Checks and Balances', in: L. Hernandez and K. Schmidt-Hebbel (eds): *Banking, Financial Integration, and International Crises*, 85–112. Santiago: Central Bank of Chile.

References

Keefer, P. and D. Stasavage (2003): 'The Limits of Delegation: Veto Players, Central Bank Independence, and the Credibility of Monetary Policy', *American Political Science Review* **97**, 3, 407–23.

Kikeri, S. (1998): *Privatization and Labor: What Happens to Workers when Governments Divest?* World Bank Technical Paper, vol. 396. Washington, DC: World Bank.

Klausen, J. (1998): *War and Welfare: Europe and the United States: 1945 to the Present.* Houndmills: Macmillan.

Knill, C. (2005): 'Introduction: Cross-National Policy Convergence: Concepts, Approaches and Explanatory Factors', *Journal of European Public Policy* **12**, 5, 764–74.

Knill, C. and D. Lehmkuhl (2007): 'An Alternative Route of European Integration: The Community's Railways Policy', *West European Politics* **23**, 1, 65–88.

Korom, P. (2013): 'Austria Inc. Forever? On the Stability of a Coordinated Corporate Network in Times of Privatization and Internationalization', *World Political Science Review* **9**, 1, 357–83.

Korpi, W. (1983): *The Democratic Class Struggle.* London: Routledge.

Köthenbürger, M., H.-W. Sinn, and J. Whalley (eds) (2006): *Privatization Experiences in the European Union.* Cambridge, MA: MIT Press.

Krajewski, M., U. Neergaard, and J. Van de Gronden (eds) (2009): *The Changing Legal Framework for Services of General Interest in Europe: Between Competition and Solidarity.* The Hague: Asser Press.

Laakso, M. and R. Taagepera (1979): 'Effective Number of Parties: A Measure with Application to West Europe', *Comparative Political Studies* **12**, 1, 3–27.

La Porta, R. and F. Lopez-de-Silanes (1999): 'The Benefits of Privatization: Evidence from Mexico', *Quarterly Journal of Economics* **114**, 4, 1193–242.

La Porta, R., F. Lopez-de-Silanes, and R. W. Vishny (1998): 'Law and Finance', *Journal of Political Economy* **106**, 6, 1113–55.

La Porta, R., F. Lopez-de-Silanes, and A. Shleifer (2002): 'Government Ownership of Banks', *Journal of Finance* **57**, 1, 265–301.

Laver, M. J. and N. Schofield (1990): *Multiparty Government: The Politics of Coalition in Europe.* Oxford: Oxford University Press.

Lee, C. K. and D. Strang (2006): 'The International Diffusion of Public-Sector Downsizing: Network Emulation and Theory-Driven Learning', *International Organization* **60**, 4, 883–910.

Leibfried, S. (2001): 'Von der Hinfälligkeit des Staates der Daseinsvorsorge: Thesen zur Zerstörung des äußeren Verteidigungsrings des Sozialstaates', in: Schader-Stiftung (ed.): *Die Zukunft der Daseinsvorsorge. Öffentliche Unternehmen im Wettbewerb*, 158–66. Darmstadt: Schader-Stiftung.

Leibfried, S., E. Huber, M. Lange, J. D. Levy, F. Nullmeier, and J. D. Stephens (eds) (2015): *The Oxford Handbook of Transformations of the State.* Oxford: Oxford University Press.

Levi-Faur, D. (2005): 'The Global Diffusion of Regulatory Capitalism', *Annals of the American Academy of Political and Social Science* **598**, 1, 12–32.

Levine, R. (1997): 'Financial Development and Economic Growth: Views and Agenda', *Journal of Economic Literature* **32**, 2, 688–726.

References

Levine, R. and S. Zervos (1998): 'Stock Markets, Banks, and Economic Growth', *American Economic Review* **88**, 3, 537–58.

Lijphart, A. (1991): 'Constitutional Choices for New Democracies', *Journal of Democracy* **2**, 1, 72–84.

Lijphart, A. (1999, 2012): *Patterns of Democracy: Government Forms and Performance in Thirty-Six Countries*. New Haven, CT: Yale University Press (2nd edition 2012).

Lind, G. (2013): 'Early Military Industry in Denmark-Norway, 1500–1814', *Scandinavian Journal of History* **38**, 4, 405–21.

Lindert, P. H. (2004): *Growing Public: Social Spending and Economic Growth since the Eighteenth Century*. Cambridge: Cambridge University Press.

Lipsey, R. G. and K. Lancaster (1956): 'The General Theory of Second Best', *Review of Economic Studies* **24**, 1, 11–32.

Loungani, P. and P. Swagel (2001): *Sources of Inflation in Developing Countries*. IMF Working Paper 01/198. Washington: IMF.

Lucas, R. E. (1973): 'Some International Evidence on Output-Inflation Tradeoffs', *American Economic Review* **63**, 3, 326–34.

Magnusson, L. and J. Ottosson (2000): 'State Intervention and the Role of History: State and Private Actors in Swedish Network Industries', *Review of Political Economy* **12**, 2, 191–205.

Majone, G. (1994): 'The Rise of the Regulatory State in Europe', *West European Politics* **17**, 3, 77–101.

Martinelli, A. (1981): 'The Italian Experience: A Historical Perspective', in: R. Vernon and Y. Aharoni (eds): *State-Owned Enterprise in the Western Economies*, 85–98. London: Croom Helm.

Mayer, F. (2006): *Vom Niedergang des unternehmerisch tätigen Staates: Privatisierungspolitik in Großbritannien, Frankreich, Italien und Deutschland*. Wiesbaden: Verlag für Sozialwissenschaften.

Megginson, W. and J. M. Netter (2001): 'From State to Market: A Survey of Empirical Studies on Privatization', *Journal of Economic Literature* **39**, 2, 321–89.

Megginson, W., R. C. Nash, J. Netter, and A. Poulsen (2004): 'The Choice of Private versus Public Capital Markets: Evidence from Privatizations', *Journal of Finance* **59**, 6, 2835–70.

Meseguer, C. (2004): 'What Role for Learning? The Diffusion of Privatisation in OECD and Latin American Countries', *Journal of Public Policy* **24**, 3, 299–325.

Meseguer, C. (2009): *Learning, Policy Making, and Market Reforms*. New York: Cambridge University Press.

Meseguer, C. and F. Gilardi (2009): 'What Is New in the Study of Policy Diffusion?', *Review of International Political Economy* **16**, 3, 527–43.

Millward, R. (2004): 'European Governments and the Infrastructure Industries, c. 1840–1915', *European Review of Economic History* **8**, 1, 3–28.

Millward, R. (2011a): 'Public Enterprise in the Modern Western World: An Historical Analysis', *Annals of Public and Cooperative Economics* **82**, 4, 375–98.

Millward, R. (2011b): 'Geo-Politics versus Market Structure Interventions in Europe's Infrastructure Industries, c. 1830–1939', *Business History* **53**, 5, 673–87.

References

Mitsopoulos, M. S. and T. Pelagidis (2009): 'Vikings in Greece: Kleptocratic Interest Groups in a Closed, Rent-Seeking Economy', *Cato Journal* 29, 2, 399–416.
Mortensen, D. T. (1970): 'Job Search, the Duration of Unemployment, and the Phillips Curve', *American Economic Review* 60, 5, 847–62.
Mueller, D. C. and P. Murrell (1986): 'Interest Groups and the Size of Government', *Public Choice* 48, 2, 125–45.
Nordhaus, W. D. (1975): 'The Political Business Cycle', *Review of Economic Studies* 42, 2, 169–90.
Noreng, O. (1981): 'State-Owned Oil Companies: Western Europe', in: R. Vernon and Y. Aharoni (eds): *State-Owned Enterprise in the Western Economies*, 133–44. London: Croom Helm.
Nowotny, E. (1986): 'Die Wirtschaftspolitik Österreichs seit 1970', in: E. Fröschl and H. Zoitl (eds): *Der österreichische Weg 1970–1985*, 37–59. Vienna: Europa Verlag.
Nybom, T. (1993): 'The Swedish Social Democratic State in a Tradition of Peaceful Revolution', in: C. Due-Nielsen, H. Kirchhoff, K. C. Lammers, and T. Nybom (eds): *Konflikt og samarbejde: Festskrift til Carl-Axel Gemzell*, 305–34. Copenhagen: Museum Tusculanums Forlag.
Obinger, H. and C. Schmitt (2011): 'Guns and Butter? Regime Competition and the Welfare State during the Cold War', *World Politics* 63, 2, 246–70.
Obinger, H. and R. Zohlnhöfer (2005): *Selling off the Family Silver: The Politics of Privatization in the OECD 1980–1990*. TransState Working Papers 15. Bremen: University of Bremen.
Obinger, H. and R. Zohlnhöfer (2007): 'Abschied vom Interventionsstaat? Der Wandel staatlicher Subventionsausgaben in den OECD-Ländern seit 1980', *Swiss Political Science Review* 13, 2, 203–36.
Obinger, H., C. Schmitt, and R. Zohlnhöfer (2014): 'Partisan Politics and Privatization in OECD Countries', *Comparative Political Studies* 47, 1294–323.
OECD (2003): *Privatising State-Owned Enterprises: An Overview of Policies and Practices in OECD Countries*. Paris: OECD.
OECD (2014): *Economic Outlook*, vol. 2. Paris: OECD Publishing.
Okten, C. and K. P. Arin (2006): 'The Effects of Privatization on Efficiency: How Does Privatization Work?', *World Development* 43, 9, 1537–56.
Olsen, J. P. (2002): 'The Many Faces of Europeanization', *Journal of Common Market Studies* 40, 5, 921–52.
Olson, M. (1982): *The Rise and Decline of Nations: Economic Growth, Stagflation, and Social Rigidities*. New Haven, CT: Yale University Press.
Perotti, E. (2013): *The Political Economy of Finance*. Social Science Research Network Working Paper 2222630.
Phelps, E. S. (1968): 'Money-Wage Dynamics and Labor-Market Equilibrium', *Journal of Political Economy* 76, 4, 678–711.
Phillips, A. W. (1958): 'The Relation between Unemployment and the Rate of Change of Money Wage Rates in the United Kingdom, 1862–1957', *Economica* 25, 100, 283–99.
Piderit, S. K. (2000): 'Rethinking Resistance and Recognizing Ambivalence: A Multidimensional View of Attitudes toward an Organizational Change', *Academy of Management Review* 25, 4, 783–94.

References

Plümper, T. and E. Neumayer (2010): 'Model Specification in the Analysis of Spatial Dependence', *European Journal of Political Research* **49**, 3, 418–42.

Polanyi, K. (1944): *The Great Transformation: The Political and Economic Origins of Our Time*. Boston, MA: Beacon Press.

Pontusson, J. (1989): 'The Triumph of Pragmatism: Nationalization and Privatization in Sweden', in: J. Vickers and V. Wright (eds): *The Politics of Privatization in Western Europe*, 129–40. London: Frank Cass.

Porter, B. D. (1994): *War and the Rise of the State: The Military Foundations of Modern Politics*. New York: Free Press.

Potrafke, N. (2012): 'Political Cycles and Economic Performance in OECD Countries: Empirical Evidence from 1951–2006', *Public Choice* **150**, 1–2, 155–79.

Privatization Barometer (2013): *The PB Report 2013: Riding the Wave*. Milano: Privatization Barometer.

Püttner, G. (1985): *Die öffentlichen Unternehmen: Ein Handbuch zu Verfassungs- und Rechtsfragen der öffentlichen Wirtschaft*. Stuttgart: Boorberg.

Quinn, D. (1997): 'The Correlates of Change in International Financial Regulation', *American Political Science Review* **91**, 3, 531–51.

Rae, D. (1968): 'A Note on the Fractionalization of Some European Party Systems', *Comparative Political Studies* **1**, 3, 413–18.

Roberts, B. M. and M. A. Saeed (2012): 'Privatizations around the World: Economic or Political Determinants?', *Economics and Politics* **24**, 1, 47–71.

Rodrik, D. (1998): 'Why Do More Open Economies Have Larger Governments?', *Journal of Political Economy* **106**, 5, 997–1032.

Rogoff, K. (1990): 'Equilibrium Political Business Cycles', *American Economic Review* **80**, 1, 21–36.

Rogoff, K. and A. Sibert (1988): 'Elections and Macroeconomic Policy Cycles', *Review of Economic Studies* **55**, 1, 1–16.

Ross, M. H. and E. Homer (1976): 'Galton's Problem in Cross-National Research', *World Politics* **29**, 1, 1–28.

Saal, D. S. and D. Parker (2001): 'Productivity and Price Performance in the Privatized Water and Sewerage Companies of England and Wales', *Journal of Regulatory Economics* **20**, 1, 61–90.

Samuelson, P. A. and R. M. Solow (1960): 'Analytical Aspects of Anti-Inflation Policy', *American Economic Review* **50**, 2, 177–94.

Sargent, T. and N. Wallace (1975): 'Rational Expectations, the Optimal Monetary Instruments, and the Optimal Money Supply Rule', *Journal of Political Economy* **83**, 2, 241–54.

Scharpf, F. W. (1999): *Regieren in Europa. Effektiv und demokratisch?* Frankfurt: Campus.

Schmidt, K. M. (2000): 'The Political Economy of Mass Privatization and the Risk of Expropriation', *European Economic Review* **44**, 2, 393–421.

Schmidt, M. G. (1996): 'When Parties Matter: A Review of the Possibilities and Limits of Partisan Influence on Public Policy', *European Journal of Political Research* **30**, 2, 155–83.

Schmitt, C. (2011): 'What Drives the Diffusion of Privatization Policy? Evidence from the Telecommunications Sector', *Journal of Public Policy* **31**, 1, 95–117.

References

Schmitt, C. (2013): 'The Janus Face of Europeanisation: Explaining Cross Sector Differences in Public Utilities', *West European Politics* **36**, 3, 547–63.

Schmitt, C. (2014a): 'The Diffusion of Privatization in Europe: Political Affinity or Economic Competition?', *Public Administration* **92**, 3, 615–35.

Schmitt, C. (2014b): 'The Employment Effects of Privatizing Public Utilities in OECD Countries', *Public Management Review* **16**, 8, 1164–83.

Schmitt, C. (2015): 'Panel Data Analysis and Partisan Effects: Why the Standard Country-Year Approach Biases against Partisan Variables', *Journal of European Public Policy* (forthcoming).

Schmitt, C. and H. Obinger (2011): 'Constitutional Barriers and the Privatization of Public Utilities in Rich Democracies', *World Political Science Review* **7**, 1, 1–24.

Schmitter, P. C. and G. Lehmbruch (1979): *Trends towards Corporatist Intermediation*. London: Sage.

Schneider, V. and F. M. Häge (2008): 'Europeanization and the Retreat of the State', *Journal of European Public Policy* **15**, 1, 1–19.

Schneider, V., S. Fink, and M. Tenbücken (2005): 'Buying out the State: A Comparative Perspective on the Privatization of Infrastructures', *Comparative Political Studies* **38**, 6, 704–27.

Schuster, P. B. (2013): 'One for All and All for One: Privatization and Universal Service Provision in the Postal Sector', *Applied Economics* **45**, 26, 3667–82.

Schuster, P. B., C. Schmitt, and S. Traub (2013): 'The Retreat of the State from Entrepreneurial Activities: A Convergence Analysis for OECD Countries, 1980–2007', *European Journal of Political Economy* **32**, 95–112.

Shapiro, C. and R. Willig (1990): 'Economic Rationales for the Scope of Privatization', in: E. N. Suleiman and J. Waterbury (eds): *The Political Economy of Public Sector Reform and Privatization*, 55–87. Boulder, CO: Westview Press.

Siaroff, A. (1999): 'Corporatism in 24 Industrial Democracies: Meaning and Measurement', *European Journal of Political Research* **36**, 2, 175–205.

Spolaore, E. (2004): 'Adjustments in Different Government Systems', *Economics and Politics* **16**, 2, 117–46.

Stevenson, D. (1999): 'War by Timetable? The Railway Race before 1914', *Past and Present* **162**, February, 163–94.

Stiefel, D. (2011): *Verstaatlichung und Privatisierung in Österreich: Illusion und Wirklichkeit*. Vienna: Böhlau.

Strange, S. (1996): *The Retreat of the State: The Diffusion of Power in the World Economy*. Cambridge: Cambridge University Press.

Tanzi, V. and L. Schuknecht (2000): *Public Spending in the 20th Century: A Global Perspective*. Cambridge: Cambridge University Press.

Taylor, J. B. (1980): 'Aggregate Dynamics and Staggered Contracts', *Journal of Political Economy* **88**, 1, 1–24.

Toninelli, P. M. (ed.) (2000): *The Rise and Fall of State-Owned Enterprise in the Western World*. Cambridge: Cambridge University Press.

Tsebelis, G. (2002): *Veto Players: How Political Institutions Work*. Princeton, NJ: Princeton University Press.

References

Vanthemsche, G. (2012): *Belgium and the Congo 1885–1980*. Cambridge: Cambridge University Press.

Verdier, D. and R. Breen (2001): 'Europeanization and Globalization Politics against Markets in the European Union', *Comparative Political Studies* **34**, 3, 227–62.

Vernon, R. (1979): 'The International Aspects of State-Owned Enterprises', *Journal of International Business Studies* **10**, 3, 7–15.

Vickers, J. and V. Wright (1989): 'The Politics of Industrial Privatization in Western Europe: An Overview', in: J. Vickers and V. Wright (eds): *The Politics of Privatization in Western Europe*, 1–30. London: Frank Cass.

Villalonga, B. (2000): 'Privatization and Efficiency: Differentiating Ownership Effects from Political, Organizational, and Dynamic Effects', *Journal of Economic Behavior and Organization* **42**, 1, 43–74.

Vogel, S. K. (1998): *Freer Markets, More Rules: Regulatory Reform in Advanced Industrial Countries*. Ithaca, NY: Cornell University Press.

Wagner, A. (1911): 'Staat (in nationalökonomischer Sicht)', in: J. Conrad, L. Elster, W. Lexis, and E. Loening (eds): *Handwörterbuch der Staatswissenschaften*, vol. 7, 727–39. Jena: Gustav Fischer.

Weiss, L. (1993): 'War, the State, and the Origins of the Japanese Employment System', *Politics and Society* **21**, 3, 325–54.

Wengenroth, U. (2000): 'The Rise and Fall of State-Owned Enterprise in Germany', in: P. M. Toninelli (ed.): *The Rise and Fall of State-Owned Enterprise in the Western World*, 103–27. Cambridge: Cambridge University Press.

Westlund, H. (1998): 'State and Market Forces in Swedish Infrastructure History', *Scandinavian Journal of History* **23**, 1–2, 65–88.

World Bank (1995): *Bureaucrats in Business: The Economics and Politics of Government Ownership*. New York: Oxford University Press.

Zohlnhöfer, R., H. Obinger, and F. Wolf (2008): 'Partisan Politics, Globalization, and the Determinants of Privatization Proceeds in Advanced Democracies (1990–2000)', *Governance* **21**, 1, 95–121.

Index

anti-trust legislation 15
autarky 12
automatic stabilizers 51

Basel III 100
beta convergence, see *convergence, of privatization policies*
bicameralism 45, 92
bipartisan model 38f

capital markets, see *financial markets*
censored data 30
civil law countries, see *legal system*
coercion, see *policy diffusion*
Cold War 25
command economy 25
common
  law countries, see *legal systems*
  market 24f
communism, collapse of 25
comparative political data set (CPDS) 45
compensation hypothesis 51
competition, see *policy diffusion*
conditional convergence, see *convergence, of privatization policies*
consensus democracies, see *democracy, models of*
constitutional
  barriers, see *constitutional, provisions*
  provisions 56, 77ff
  regulations, see *constitutional, provisions*
convergence
  of privatization policies 70ff
  criteria of Treaty of Maastricht 34
corporatism 45f
costs,
  fixed, see *monopoly, natural*
  sunk, see *monopoly, natural*

Daseinsvorsorge 15ff, also see *public utilities*
Democracy, models of 43f
departmental agency, definition of 57f
deregulation, see *regulation*
determinants of privatization 26ff, 70ff
diffusion, see *policy diffusion*

economic
  development 9, 11, 15, 20, 36
  integration 51f
  performance 27ff
  problem pressure, see *economic, performance*
economies of scale, see *monopoly, natural*
efficiency
  hypothesis 51
  microeconomic 29
  macroeconomic, see *gross domestic product, growth*
elections, effect on privatization programmes 37ff, 84
electoral system 43ff
employers' associations 41f
employment
  effect of privatization, see *unemployment*
  Employment Index (IPEe) 32, 62, 71ff, 85
emulation, see *policy diffusion*
endogeneity problem 31, 48, 50, 56, 85
error correction model (ECM) 32, 73f
European
  Commission 52
  integration, see *Europeanization*
  monetary union (EMU) 96
Europeanization 52f, 70
event history analysis (EHA) 34

federalism 45f, 92
financial
  crisis 98ff
  markets 25, 46ff
  openness 51f
foreign direct investment (FDI) 51
fragmentation of governments 44
functionalist theory 26

Galton's problem 53
geographical proximity 55, 91
globalization 24f, 51f, 86, 96
Golden Age 21ff, 60
Great
  Depression 16, 38, 94
  Recession, see *financial, crisis*

Index

gross domestic product (GDP)
  level of, see *economic development*
  growth 15, 24, 27, 30ff, 54f, 76, 86

ideology, see *party preferences*
index of public involvement 31
index of public entrepreneurship 40, 58ff, 74, 82, 89ff
industrialization 7ff, 94
inflation 35f
interdependence 53ff, 90
interest groups 41f
international diffusion, see *policy diffusion*
internet 24

Keynesianism 23

learning, see *policy diffusion*
legal system 46f
Liberalism 25, 103
liberalization 23, 45, 50, 52, 97, 103

majoritarian democracy, see *democracy, models of*
market failure 15, 19
mass privatization 39
median voter 39
mixed economy 21, 25
monarch 6f
monopoly,
  fiscal 7, 14, 20
  natural 7, 15, 21, 24
  power 36
multicollinearity 35, 55

nationalization 7ff, 41, 98f
neo-liberalism, see *liberalism*
network-based,
  utilities 7ff, 21, 24, 52, 64, 66ff, 77ff
nominal rigidities, theory of 38

oil shock 16, 23ff, 95
omitted variable bias 35

path dependency 43, 70
partisan theory (PT) 37ff, 45, 84f
party preferences, see *partisan theory*
Phillips curve 37
plurality voting, see *democracy, models of*
policy
  diffusion 40, 53ff, 89ff
  legacy 49f
political business cycle theory (PBCT) 37
political constraints index (POLCON) 45
population growth 7
post-war consensus 25, 38
power resource theory 41

presidentalism 44f
privatization
  ban 48, 56
  formal, definition of 57f
  substantial, definition of 57f
procrastination 44
property rights 46
proportional representation, see *democracy, models of*
public
  budget deficit 23, 33ff, 76, 85
  corporation, definition of 57f
  debt 33ff, 74, 85, 103
  utilities, see *network-based utilities*

rational expectations 37f
referenda 45
regulation, also see *constitutional, provisions*
  of capital markets 46
  of industries and services 13, 30, 48ff, 79, 97
resistance to change 41
REST database 32
Revenue Index 32ff, 62ff, 71ff, 85ff

sample selection bias 30, 49
Second World War 12ff
services publics 30, 146, also see *network-based utilities*
sigma convergence, see *convergence, of privatization policies*
single European market 41, 52
social
  rights 48, 79
  view of privatization 36
spatial
  diffusion, see *policy diffusion*
  econometrics 31, 49, 89ff
stagflation 23ff, 38, 96
state
  company, definition of 57f
  duties, see *state, principles*
  principles 48, 79
status-quo bias 42, 45
strikes 42
subsidies 21ff, 54
supply-side economics 29

taxation 7, 29
technological,
  change 7, 24ff, 94
  progress, see *technological, change*
trade
  openness 51f, 71ff, 92
  relations 91
Treaty of Maastricht 24, 33f, 55, 85
two-party system 38, 43

Index

unemployment 23, 29, 35, 37f, 55
unions 17, 41ff, 76, 82ff
universal service 22, 56
urbanization 7, 19, 94

veto player theory 45ff, 56

war of attrition 44
weighting matrix, see *spatial econometrics*
welfare state regime 54
Westminster model, see *democracy, models of*
winset 45